1

Many many thanks to Anne Lloyd for identification and allocation of photographs; Nick Nicholson – my inestimable number one manuscript consultant with an amazingly vast knowledge of the subject matter; Dev Ann Rouen for functioning as my objective proofreader; and Ilya Grigoriev for his invaluable assistance at the State Archives of the Russian Federation!

2

Journal of a Russian Grand Duchess:

Complete Annotated 1913 Diary of Olga Romanov, Eldest Daughter of the Last Tsar

Introduction to the Young Grand Duchess

One of the best ways to get to know a historical person is by reading their own writings. This is very much the case with the eldest daughter of the last Tsar of Russia, the Grand Duchess Olga Nikolaevna Romanova. The Grand Duchess's own diary recordings certainly give the reader a remarkable insight into the private world of the Russian imperial family, as well as to her own personal thoughts and observations.

Who was the Grand Duchess Olga? The large baby girl came into the world on November 15 (Old Style[1]: November 3) 1895, in St. Petersburg, Russia. On that day her father, Tsar Nicholas II, wrote in his diary: "A day I will remember forever . . . at exactly 9 o'clock a baby's cry was heard and we all breathed a sigh of relief! With prayer we named the daughter sent to us by God 'Olga'!"

Olga's aunt, the Grand Duchess Ksenia Alexandrovna wrote a somewhat more pragmatic diary entry on November 3: "The birth of a daughter to Nicky and

---

[1] The Gregorian calendar (new style) replaced the Julian calendar (old style) in Catholic countries beginning in 1582. This change was also implemented in Protestant and Orthodox countries after a significant delay. In Russia the change took place after the revolution in 1918.

Alix! A great joy, although it's a great pity it's not a son![2] The baby is huge—

weighing 10 pounds—and had to be pulled out with forceps!"

Baby Olga with her parents

The Grand Duchess Olga Nikolaevna Romanova was the first of Tsar

Nicholas II's and Tsarina Alexandra Feodorovna's five children. She was born at

the Anichkov Palace, her father's childhood home where the newlywed imperial

---

[2] At this time Salic law prevented any female from inheriting the Russian throne unless all direct male heirs were gone. Hence, Olga was not considered the heir apparent, even though she was the first born child of the Tsar.

couple initially settled, sharing the palace with Nicholas's mother, the Dowager Empress Maria Feodorovna.

The baby Grand Duchess's birth was regarded as "in the purple"— taking place during the imperial reign of her parents. Her Russian title "Velikaya Knyazhna" is most precisely translated as "The Grand Princess," which means that Olga, as an "Imperial Highness," was higher in rank than other princesses in Europe who were merely "Royal Highnesses." "Grand Duchess" is the more common English translation, which is used in this book.

Olga's mother Alexandra startled her own grandmother, Queen Victoria of England, by insisting on breastfeeding her firstborn, which was quite unusual for aristocratic, let alone royal, women in the nineteenth century. Ksenia Alexandrovna once again recorded on November 5: "Alix[3] started feeding [Olga] herself. During dinner, the wet-nurse's son started to take her breast, and we all took turns to go in and watch the spectacle!"

Olga was the only of her siblings to meet in person her formidable English great-grandmother, who was also one of her godmothers. The tiny Grand Duchess was too young to remember her visit to the British court, as it occurred during the family's trip abroad when she was just an infant. The old Queen was delighted to meet her new great-granddaughter and spend time with her, posing for photographs.

---

[3] The Tsarina was known to her family as "Alix".

Queen Victoria was delighted to meet her new great-granddaughter. Left to right: Alexandra with baby Olga on her lap, Nicholas II, Queen Victoria and Edward, the Prince of Wales.

As baby Olga grew into a toddler in 1897, she became big sister to another imperial daughter, Tatiana. Later in her diary Olga would refer to herself and her sister Tatiana as "We 2." The two girls were very close in age, did most activities together, and were often dressed in matching outfits.

Olga as a toddler with her baby sister Tatiana

In 1899, Olga and Tatiana were joined by yet another baby sister, Maria. In 1901, just before the imperial family went on a holiday to Peterhof, a seaside town on the Gulf of Finland founded by Peter the Great, Olga came down with typhoid fever. This was the same disease that killed her great-grandfather Prince Albert, Queen Victoria's consort. The six-year-old Grand Duchess, seriously ill for five long weary weeks, was nursed by her mother. For a while it seemed that Olga might not recover, but she did.

Olga, Tatiana and Maria

Olga was still in bed when her youngest sister, Anastasia, was born in June. The little Grand Duchess was very disappointed at not being able to attend her new baby sister's baptism, which would have been her first "official" ceremony.

The four sisters collectively referred to themselves as "OTMA," an acronym for the first four letters of their respective given names: Olga, Tatiana, Maria, and Anastasia. Olga and Tatiana were known to their family and friends as "The Big Pair", while Maria and Anastasia were "The Little Pair".

OTMA

Eventually the growing family made the relatively small Alexander Palace in Tsarskoe Selo[4] their permanent home. As the imperial family kept expanding, Olga's parents did their best to provide "normal" lives for their daughters. Just like any other Russian family they celebrated Orthodox holidays such as Christmas by exchanging gifts and decorating a fir tree.

Margaret Eagar, who had worked as the girls' governess since 1898, remembered in her memoirs one particular Christmas when the young grand duchesses were delighted to see their mother magnificently attired for a ceremony. They circled around her in speechless admiration when suddenly

---

[4] Literally translated as "The Imperial Village," a St. Petersburg suburb

Olga clapped her hands, and exclaimed fervently, "Oh! Mama - you are just like a lovely Christmas tree!"

Olga (far right) with her three sisters at Christmas time

The children made Christmas and birthday presents for their parents with their own hands, usually needlework. One Christmas, despite Eagar's attempts to convince her otherwise, Olga insisted on making a kettle-holder for her father. It had a picture of a little kettle singing on a fire, around which she embroidered a blue frame, and the little girl was very happy with her accomplishment. When Christmas came, she presented it to her father, saying, "Nanny was afraid that it wasn't going to be of much use to you because it's a kettle-holder, but you can put it on your table and use it as a placemat, or hang it on the wall as a picture. Just look at the pretty little frame around it."

From many intimate anecdotes told by her governess, we get a glimpse of Olga's mentality as a little girl. Especially revealing is Olga's attitude about her status as the oldest imperial sibling. The little Grand Duchess was always profoundly interested in biblical stories, like the one of Joseph and his brothers. After Eagar pronounced how terrible it was for the brothers to be so jealous and so cruel to their youngest sibling, Olga responded, "Joseph was not the eldest, and the beautiful coat should have been given to the eldest son; the other brothers knew that, and perhaps that was why they threw him in the pit." All explanations were useless—Olga's sympathies lay with Joseph's eldest brother, Reuben.

Young Olga and Tatiana in Russian court dresses

A similar incident occurred when a cinematograph was played for the children and some of their friends. The film showed two little girls playing in a garden, when the older one attempted to snatch a toy from the younger one, who refused to give it up. Foiled in her attempts, the elder girl seized a spoon and pounded the little one with it, which made the latter quickly relinquish the toy and begin to cry. Tatiana was upset and weeping to see the poor little girl so ill-treated, but Olga said, "I am sure that the toy originally belonged to the big sister, and she was kind and lent it to her sister; then she wanted it back, and the little sister would not give it up, so she had to beat her."

When the book "Alice in Wonderland" was first read to Olga, she was horrified at the manners of the queens. "No queens," Olga said, "would ever be so rude." From books and stories Olga was also able to learn some things about the outside world that she had never experienced firsthand. When the "Alice in Wonderland" chapter about Alice's journey by railway was read to her, she was very amused that Alice did not have the train compartment all to herself. It was explained to her that each person had to buy a ticket and occupy just one seat in the train, with some tickets costing more than others and the highest-priced tickets granting a better place in the train. Still bemused, Olga asked, "When you travel, can anyone with the same kind of ticket you have get into the same carriage as you do?" No matter how normal her parents tried to make Olga's life, many mundane things that most people took for granted were completely foreign concepts to her.

Even as a child Olga tended to be the most reflective and analytical of her siblings. When she was eight years old, the war between Russia and Japan broke out in 1904. All the girls, even the three-year-old Anastasia, worked hard at frame knitting, making scarves for the soldiers, and the two eldest girls also crocheted caps. One day Olga, diligently at work on her crocheting, suddenly said to Mrs. Eagar, "I hope the Russian soldiers will kill all the Japanese; not leave even one alive." When the governess explained that there were many innocent children and women in Japan, people who could not fight, Olga reflected for a moment. She then asked if they also had an emperor in Japan, and hearing that they did, she continued to ask various other questions about Japan. After a pause, Olga finally said slowly, "I did not know that the [Japanese] were people just like ourselves and not like monkeys." After that conversation, Olga never again said anything about being pleased to hear of the deaths of the Japanese.

Olga and her bicycle

When she started to read herself, one of Olga's favorite subjects was stories about medieval European history. According to Eagar, Olga once read a story about the execution of the Welsh Prince Llewellyn. The English beheaded him, sending his head to London, which made a great impression on the little girl. She was terribly shocked, and exclaimed, "It was a good thing he was dead before they cut off his head; it would have hurt him most awfully if he was alive." The governess explained that they were not always so kind and usually cut the heads off living people, to which Olga replied, "I really think people are much better now than they used to be. I'm very glad that I live now when people are so kind."

Olga in a sailor suit

According to her governess, Olga was taught by masters of music as well as Russian and mathematics. Once her arithmetic master, who was a professor of algebra from one of the universities, assigned Olga to write something; she asked his permission to go see the Russian master, who was teaching Tatiana in the next room. When asked why she needed to see him, Olga told him that she wanted to ask him how to spell "arithmetic." The math teacher then spelled this difficult word for her, to which she declared with great admiration, "How clever you are! And how hard you must have studied to be able not only to count so well but to spell such very long words!"

One of Olga's lesson notebooks

Pierre Gilliard, the grand duchesses' French tutor, described in his memoirs his first meeting with Olga: "The eldest of the Grand Duchesses, Olga, a girl of about ten, [was] very blonde, with eyes full of mischief, and a slightly retroussé little nose; [she] was studying me with an expression that seemed like an attempt to find my weakest point— however, from this child emanated such feeling of purity and sincerity that she immediately gained my sympathy."

Aleksei, their long-awaited brother and heir to the Russian throne was born in 1904, bringing elation to the imperial family and the entire country. But the little boy who was destined to become the next Tsar of Russia was born with a rare and untreatable blood disorder - hemophilia. The baby's condition brought the tight-knit imperial family even closer together, but understandably became the source of severe anxieties for Olga's parents. Her little son's ailment had a serious effect on Alexandra's own health, and she herself developed frequent illnesses from stress about Aleksei's wellbeing.

Olga (far right) and all her siblings holding their kittens on the imperial yacht

Unfortunately, growing desperation over Aleksei's hemophilia also contributed to the Tsar and Tsarina's dependence on the charismatic Siberian peasant Grigori Rasputin, whim they believed to be a faith healer—a factor of major historical significance. Although Rasputin's influence on the imperial couple was highly exaggerated, this unfortunate attachment is believed to eventually severely damage Nicholas's reputation as a ruler, which forced his abdication.

Olga with her sisters, brother and their beloved "Mama"

One of the most famous rulers of Russia was Empress Catherine the Great, so why could not Olga, as the eldest daughter of the tsar, inherit the throne? The answer goes back several generations. After the death of his mother, Catherine's son, Tsar Paul I, quickly instated the Salic law because of his hatred toward the late empress. Paul wanted to prevent any other woman from ruling Russia again. If it were not for the Salic law, the eldest imperial daughter would have been recognized as the heir presumptive and become empress in the absence of a legitimate male heir.

Grand Duchess Olga on one of the imperial yachts

Meanwhile, due to the Tsarina's frequent illnesses, it often fell to Olga - as she grew older - to perform the duties that the Tsar's consort would usually do. Of all the imperial children Olga was closest to her father, but she loved both her parents profoundly, as is evident from her diary. Olga was certainly greatly sympathetic toward her mother, especially when it came to Alexandra's health.

Olga with her little brother Aleksei

Much like her father, Olga enjoyed taking long walks in the parks of Tsarskoe Selo. She often said that she would someday like to live in a small village because she liked nature much more than the city. Olga also loved to sail on the imperial yacht Standart, and greatly enjoyed the annual summer trips to the Black Sea in the Crimea, as well as other family holidays to Finland, Poland and Germany.

As Olga grew older, in addition to her love of nature and the outdoors, she became an even more voracious reader of books: the classics, the history of Russia and works detailing the lives of the peasants, ancient traditions, customs, laws, and geography of her nation. According to Meriel Buchanan, she had an extraordinary memory and never forgot anything she learned or had been told.

Olga also loved music and was an excellent pianist. Along with her siblings, the Grand Duchess had keen interest in the lives and problems of others. It was she who once noticed a disabled girl in one of the keepers' cottages in the park at Tsarskoe Selo and insisted on becoming the child's "sponsor." She made arrangements for the little girl to be transported to a hospital, and planned on paying for her care out of her own allowance.

Olga (right) and Tatiana (left) with their first cousin Irina, daughter of Ksenia
Alexandrovna

In her memoirs, Meriel Buchanan, daughter of the English ambassador to
Russia, described the physical appearance of the fifteen-year-old Olga at an
imperial ball in 1910: "That evening . . . [Olga] wore a pale pink chiffon dress of
almost classical simplicity, a silver ribbon was bound round her golden hair,
which was parted in the middle, and her only jewels were a string of pearls round
her slender neck. She had not the regular features, the almost mystical beauty of
her sister, Tatiana Nikolaevna, but with her rather tip-tilted nose, her wide
laughing mouth, her sparkling blue eyes, she had a charm, freshness, an
enchanting exuberance that made her irresistible."

The "Big Pair" on a beach with Anna Vyrubova, a close family friend

In November 1911 Olga turned sixteen, which was considered the coming of age for Russian aristocratic girls. Every young girl impatiently awaited this first "grown-up" ball, her coming out to the world and transitioning into adulthood. A grand dinner and gala party was taking place on that day at the palace at Livadia in the Crimea, to celebrate Olga's birthday. Those who received the following invitation considered it to be a great honor:

"Their Imperial Majesties invite [You] to dinner and a dancing party to be held on Thursday November 3rd, at 6:45 in the evening, at the Livadia Palace."

Dress for the occasion was strictly regulated:

"Military cavaliers in frock coat with epaulets. . . . Civilians in evening dress with white tie."

Olga on her sixteenth birthday, wearing a pink dress

General Alexander Spiridovich, the Chief of Secret Personal Police in charge of protecting the imperial family, described the gala: "Dinner was served on small tables. Many candles, silver, flowers. At the round table in the center were seated Their Majesties, Grand Dukes Nicholas Nikolaevich, Pierre Nikolaevich, Alexander Mikhailovich, George Mikhailovich, with their wives, and the Minister of the Court. The star of the party, Olga Nikolaevna, in a pink dress, for the first time with her hair in a chignon, presided over the table. Her escort was N. P. Sablin. Still a young girl, very naïve, she often asked her escort what she should do. . . . All flushed in the face, charming in her pink dress, Olga Nikolaevna literally beamed with joy at the great favor accorded to her regiment[5]. They congratulated her and kissed her hand."

Olga in her Elizavetgrad Hussar uniform, of which she was very proud

Unlike her younger sister Maria, Olga did not often talk about wanting a husband and lots of children. However, it is evident from her diary that she was a

---

[5] The 9th Hussar regiment of Elizavetgrad, of which Olga was the chief

very romantic young woman, who often idealized the officers she inevitably developed crushes on.

After Olga turned eighteen, several royal young men started to be considered as potential husbands for her. Among them were her cousin Grand Duke Dimitri Pavlovich; Prince Arthur of Connaught; the Duke of Leuchtenberg; and even briefly Edward, the Prince of Wales, the future Duke of Windsor.

In the meantime, Olga continued to meet handsome officers with whom she unsurprisingly fell in love. A Crimean researcher Maria Zemlyanichenko, one of the earliest scholars who read Olga's 1913 diary, was the first to take notice of the recurring abbreviation "S.," which referred to the name of Olga's one such romantic interest. Upon closer inspection this seemed to be a letter referring to a person's nickname rather than to their given name. Knowing that the imperial family liked to use affectionate nicknames for each other, like "Sunny" or "Sunshine," we can speculate that this letter may have stood for something similar. Her beloved became her "Sweet One," who brought happiness into her world. Different codes, or abbreviations referred to Olga's other love interests.

Through her 1913 journal we follow Olga's "crushes" as they become real psychological attachments: she longs to see "him" all the time, be near "him", misses "him." And she is always full of happiness when she does see her "dear one" and "precious one." When Olga's diary was compared to other documents, it was possible to figure out some of the names of the mysterious love interests and secret codes. All of Olga's code language in 1913 diary was decoded and is included in this book.

Olga (left) next to Pavel Voronov, the officer with whom she fell in love. In her 1913 diary, the Grand Duchess referred to Voronov as "S.", which was probably an abbreviation for "Sweet One". "S." later married someone else, which devastated Olga.

Olga started recording her thoughts and daily activities in a personal journal around the age of ten in 1905, in accordance with the imperial family tradition. She kept these journals until March 1917, around the time of her father's abdication from the Russian throne. All of the Grand Duchess's original diaries are currently held at GARF (State Archives of Russian Federation) in Fond # 673, op. 1, 271 ed. The documents contained in this Fond are dated 1895–1917. Fond #673 contains additional documents which reflect the Grand Duchess's other activities, connected to her work at the infirmary, her patronage of various committees, military regiments of which she was chief, as well as her correspondence with relatives and friends. The journals however, are arguably the most valuable of these documents.

Twelve of Olga's diary books survived intact. From 1905 until 1912 they are custom-made memorial gift books, 9 x 13 inches (22.86 x 33.02 cm), a different color for each year, in silk bindings, with the dates on the cover. From 1913 until 1916 they are contained in large notebooks with dark leather bindings, which fit the entire year plus a few months of the next. The entire 1910 diary is missing—probably destroyed by Olga herself after the revolution. All the journals consist of short entries about regular events, activities, and meetings kept daily during the year. Only during the early years do we see some missed entries.

This book comprises the complete original translations, as well as annotations, of the Grand Duchess's 1913 diary. The translations were made directly from the facsimiles of Olga's diary pages, which makes this an important primary source for imperial Russia and Romanov scholars.

The 1913 journal is a unique diary-travelogue blend – not only does Grand Duchess Olga tell about her daily pursuits and romantic interests, she also describes her trips on the imperial yacht to destinations like Finland, Crimea, Peterhof and Moscow. And since the year 1913 also marked the tercentennial, the latter part of the diary contains full description of the pageantries and celebrations during the family's pilgrimage to ancient Russian cities like Vladimir, Suzdal and Novgorod – the birth places of Romanov Dynasty.

Page from Olga's 1913 original journal, dated "Sunday, 24 November"

Unbeknownst to the young Grand Duchess, 1913 turned out to be the last full year of peace for Russia and the world: the First World War broke out the following year, bringing the fatal revolution in its wake. As a result Olga's father, Tsar Nicholas II abdicated his throne in March of 1917, and Olga and her family were placed under house arrest. Only a few short months after that, they were exiled to Siberia and ultimately the Urals.

Olga's short life story ended tragically: she and her entire family were brutally executed by the Bolsheviks, who in October of 1917 seized power from the more moderate Provisional Government. The Grand Duchess was twenty two years old at the time of her murder.

Although "Journal of a Russian Grand Duchess" stands on its own, this book may also be considered a direct prequel to "The Diary of Olga Romanov: Royal Witness to the Russian Revolution" by Helen Azar. The latter consists of Olga's diaries and letters during the war years (1914-1917), which covers the period of her work as a Sister of Mercy at military infirmaries.

The following titles by Helen Azar may also be of interest to the reader:

- "*Russia's Last Romanovs: In Their Own Words*"
- "*Maria and Anastasia: The Youngest Romanov Grand Duchesses In Their Own Words*"

The Romanov Dynasty's Tercentennial insignia

January

1 January, 1913. Tuesday. Tsarskoe Selo. At 10 1/2 [we] went to the
regimental church for obednya[6]. Otetz[7] Alexander Vasiliev served. After [we]
returned, had breakfast with Papa and Sergei T. Mama did not get up yet,
because she has a severe headache and is tired. At 2 o'cl. 15 min. we four[8]
walked with Papa. Almost no snow at all, but it is 5 deg.[rees][9] below [zero]. At 3
1/2 o'clock Papa went to the Grand Palace[10] to receive the escort and diplomats,
while we went to see Countess Hendrikova[11]. Sat with her for a while, and then
went to [see] Aunt Mops[12], and from there to Anya's[13]. N.P.[14] was there. We had
tea all together, it was awfully cozy. Returned at 5 o'cl.[ock], Mama was lying
down on the sofa in her study. It was very dark there and I think she was
sleeping. Papa returned after 5 o'cl. and we had tea together. He went to
Grandmama's[15] in Petersburg for dinner. We four had dinner with Anya and

---

[6] Holy liturgy

[7] Otetz – literally "Father" mraning a priest

[8] When Olga said "we 4" or "we four" she was referring to all four sisters. "We 5" includes Aleksei. Likewise, when she wrote "we 2", it meant just her and Tatiana.

[9] Olga used Celscius for temperature measure

[10] Aka The Catherine Palace in Tsarskoe Selo

[11] Mother of Anastasia "Nastenka" Hendrikova, lady in waiting at court and Olga's close friend

[12] Eugenia Maximilianovna, Duchess of Leuchtenberg, mother of "Uncle Petya" and mother-in-law of Grand Duchess Olga Alexandrovna.

[13] Anna Vyrubova, close friend of the imperial family

[14] Nikolai Pavlovich Sablin, the Tsar's aide-de-camp

[15] Dowager Empress Maria Feodorovna, the Tsar's mother

Mama in the mauve room[16]. She still has a headache, and heart No. 2[17]. After

dinner she was lying down on the sofa there, and we sat near by on the floor and

worked. [I] prayed with Aleksei as usual at 8 o'cl. Went to bed at 10 o'cl. The

year started out well – no one knows how it will end. Oh Lord, save Papa, Mama

and all.

Wednesday. 2 January. At 10 ½ we four went to the lower regimental church for

obednya with Papa and Aunt Olga. Today is this church's and the regiment's

holiday. Otetz Alexander did the service. Then there was a moleben by Otetz

Georgi Schavelsky. Aunt Ksenia[18] and Irina[19] had breakfast, and Irina stayed

until 9 o'cl. Mama had breakfast in her bedroom as she still has a headache and

does not feel well. Her heart is enlarged and beating fast. She says she has an

elastic heart. May the Lord help her get better! At 2 1/2 Aunt Ksenia left, and we

four walked with Papa, Aunt Olga[20] and Irina. 4 degrees below in the afternoon.

We walked around the park and then in Bablovo[21]. After that we walked around

the big pond. [I] constantly fought with Anastasia and Maria. Had tea with Papa,

Mama and Irina. The same had dinner. Prayed with Aleksei. At night [I] sat at

---

[16] Empress Alexandra's sitting room at the Alexander Palace

[17] Alexandra devised a numeric scale for pain, 1 being the lowest.

[18] Grand Duchess Ksenia Alexandrovna, the Tsar's sister.

[19] Princess Irina Alexandrovna, the daughter of Grand Duchess Ksenia, Princess Irina Alexandrovna, Olga's first cousin.

[20] Grand Duchess Olga Alexandrovna, the Tsar's sister.

[21] Possibly Olga was referring to the Bablovo Palace or park opposite the main ate of The Catherine Palace park.

Mama's and knitted until 10 o'cl. Anya was there too and Papa came later. The little ones went to bed earlier.

Grand Duchess Olga Nikolaevna

Thursday. 3 January. Of course [I] got up late. At 10 o'cl. [we] tried on the Russian dresses[22]. After that we four rode in a carriage with Trina. Had breakfast with Papa. Mama stayed in her [room] and got up only for tea because she still does not fell well: has a headache, heart is enlarged and is very tired. In the

---

[22] Embroidered court gowns

afternoon we four walked with Papa. Slid down the hill by the regimental church near the pond and then by the white tower. It was lots of fun, and we were laughing a lot. Had tea with Papa and Mama. The same had dinner. Madame Zizi[23] sat in my [room] until tea. I played the piano for a while before dinner, wrote letters and did not do anything else in particular. In the evening Mama felt better than in the morning, thank God. We sat and worked. Papa read. Anya was here.

Friday. 4 January. We four rode with Trina[24]. Mama did not sleep well and is feeling poorly. Had breakfast with Papa and dear General Dumbadze[25]. At 2 o'cl. 7 min. Tatiana, Lili Obolenskaya[26] and I went to Grandmama's in Petersburg. We stayed there for about an hour and then went to Aunt Olga's with Irina. Had tea there with her, Aunt Ksenia, Aunt Minnie[27] and Madame Steckel with her daughter Zoya. Stayed there until 6 o'cl. It was lots of fun. After that Zoya, Irina and I went to her [house]. Later returned with Olga Yevgenievna[28] at 7 o'cl. 15 min. Prayed with Aleksei as usual. Had dinner and spent the evening with Papa and Mama. N.P. left for Sevastopol[29] tonight. May the Lord save him.

---

[23] Elizabeth Naryshkina, one of ladies-in-waiting

[24] Catherine Schneider, one of the tutors at the imperial court

[25] Ivan Antonovich Dumbadze: Major-General of the Tsar's Retinue

[26] Princess Elizabeth Nikolaevna Obolenskaya – a lady at court

[27] H.I.H. Grand Duchess Maria Georgievna, wife of Grand Duke Georgi Mikhailovch, an imperial cousin

[28] Olga Yevgenyevna Byutsova, Alexandra's lady-in-waiting

[29] City in the Crimea

Catherine "Trina" Schneider

Saturday. 5 January. Until 11 ½ o'cl. before obednya, sat at Mama's and knitted. She was lying down with her eyes closed. She did no feel well: pale, heart is not enlarged but she is tired. After obednya and moleben[30] had breakfast with Papa and Aunt Olga. 10 degrees below in the afternoon. We four walked with them. Mama was lying down on the sofa at tea. Her hair was not made so she wore a lace shawl on her head. We were invited to the regimental church for the vsenoshnaya[31]. It was awfully nice. Had dinner with Papa and Aunt Olga next to Mama's sofa. She was feeling better in the evening. Thank God! [We] sat with

[30] Prayer service for Intercession.

[31] Evening Vigil prayer

her and worked. Papa read in his [room]. Anya came over at about 10 o'cl. She seemed happy. [I] went to bed at 10 1/2.

Sunday. 6 January. At 10 o'cl. 20 min Papa left for Petersburg. At 10 ½ [we] went to the regimental church for obednya. [We] stayed in the chapel. We four had breakfast by ourselves. After that [we] sat with Mama for about an hour. She felt weak and did not sleep well. At 2 o'cl. 7 min we 2 went to Irina's in Petersburg with Olga Yevgenyevna. Zoya Steckel and Sasha Leuchtenberg[32] were there. She is awfully nice. We did not do anything in particular but had lots of fun. We 5 had tea and laughed a lot. Returned at 7 o'cl. 15 min.. Prayed with Aleksei. Had dinner with Papa and Mama and spent the evening together. She is still not feeling very well, but better than in the morning, thank God.

---

[32] H.I. H. Alexander Georgievich Romanovsky- Leuchtenberg, 7th Duke of Leuchtenberg

"Mama"

Monday. 7 January. Lessons started today. French first, then Russian. I was supposed to have God's Word lesson, but Batushka did not show up. Drawing was last. Had breakfast downstairs with Papa, Mama and Aunt Minnie[33]. Mama was lying down on the sofa. [She] does not feel well at all. It is cold and snowing today. We 4 walked in the garden with Papa. Aunt Olga arrived at 4 o'cl. 15 min. and we 5 went to the Christmas party with her and Papa for the officers of the guard and Svodny Regiment in the Round Hall. Aunt Olga was giving out gifts. After that she and I went to talk to the officers of the guard. It was terribly awkward. I spoke with my friend AKSHV [34]. for the first time. Was so happy. After

[33] Grand Duchess Maria Georgievna, wife of Grand Duke Georgi Mikailovich.

[34] Most likely Olga used this code for Alexander Konstantinovich Shvedov, an officer in her father's Escort Guard who was her romantic interest at the time.

5 o'cl. we 2 drove in a motor with Trina for the physics lesson. When [we] returned, I did homework for tomorrow. After that I had a music lesson. We 2 had dinner with Papa and Count Grabbe. Spent the evening at Mama's Anya was also there. Papa read in his [room]. Mama still does not feel well.

Tuesday. 8 January. Had lessons: English, French, History and Russian. Had breakfast with Papa and Uncle Pavel[35]. Mama did not get up until tea time. Her heart is No.2 and she does not feel well. Lord, save us. In the afternoon T[atiana], M[aria] and I walked with Papa. It was 5 degrees below and [there was] a bit more snow. Then we did [homework] exercises and had a dance lesson. We did not have a German lesson because the teacher was ill. Had dinner with Papa and Petrovsky. Mama stayed in her [room]. Her heart was beating fast and she did not feel well. We sat with her and Anya in the evening. Papa read in his [room]. Went to bed after 10 o'cl.

[35] Grand Duke Pavel Alexandrovich, one of the Tsar's uncles.

Olga,Tatiana, Maria and Aleksei (carried by an officer) by the regimental church

Wednesday. 9 January. Had 2 history lessons: Russian History and World History. There was no German lesson. Did not have lessons in the afternoon, since we were supposed to go to Grandmama's for a Christmas Party, but did not go because Aunt Ksenia and Vasia[36] have the flu. Had breakfast with Papa. Mama got up only for tea. She is still not feeling well - her heart or her head. In

---

[36] H.I. H. Prince Vasily, one of Ksenia Alexandrovna's sons.

the afternoon we 4 walked with Papa. The weather was wonderful: 13 degrees below, bright sun, sky and moon. Slid down the hill by the white tower. Had tea with Papa and Mama. Before dinner T.[atiana] and I played the piano in four hands. After that prayed with Aleksei. In the evening sat at Mama's. Papa read in his [room] and came over to Mama's [room] after 10 o'cl.[ock]. Anya and I helped her paste photographs into the album and knitted. Went to bed after 10 o'clock.

Thursday. 10 January. This morning I had English, French, Russian and drawing lessons. Had breakfast and dinner with Papa and Veselkin[37]. Mama slept a bit in the afternoon, and she has a headache and is very tired. At 2 ½ o'cl. we 4 went up to the big hill in the garden and slid down on spades and flat wooden sleds. It was lots of fun. There is almost no snow so it is extremely slippery. Papa received the Mongolian delegation, which is why he came later, and we 2 walked around the garden with him for a bit. The weather is sunny and cold. Had tea with Papa, Mama and Aunt Marie Al.[exandrovna?]. After that had a German lesson. In the evening helped Anya paste photographs into the album. Mama came later, she is still not feeling well.

Friday. 11 January. World History, Russian, English and Russian History lessons. Had tea with Papa, Kostya[38] and general Rennenkampf, commander of the 3rd Corps. In the afternoon we 4 slid down the hill and [skated] on ice rink with Papa. It was lots of fun. The weather is cold, clear. Had French Reading and

---

[37] Probably the Tsar's aide-de-camp.

[38] H.H. Prince Konstantin Konstantinovich of Russia, son of Grand Duke Konstantin, a Romanov cousin.

Music lessons. Mama got up for tea and was lying down on the sofa. Papa had dinner with the Cuirassiers, and we 4 had dinner with Mama. Her head was [feeling] fine thank God, and she was a happy angel! Went to bed after 10. Anya came over. Prayed with Aleksei at 8 o'clock.

Saturday. 12 January. Moleben[39] at 1 ½ o'cl. Papa received. Had breakfast with him, Aunt Olga and Sasha V.[40] Mama has a headache again, and she stayed in bed until tea. In the afternoon we 4 played on the ice rink with Papa, Aunt Olga and Sasha V. and slid down the hill. It is warmer today, and it's snowing. Had tea with Papa, Mama, Aunt Olga and Irina. Went to vsenoshnaya at the regimental church. The Cossacks were there as the choir singers are sick with scarlet fever. Had dinner with Papa, Irina, Sasha V. and Anya. Mama was in her room on the sofa. In the evening we sat with her and worked. Anya was pasting photographs into the album. N.P. came back today. Went to bed at about 10 o'cl.

Sunday. 13 January. At 10 ½ we went to obednya at the regimental church, the Cossacks sang. Had a big Sunday breakfast: Commanders from the local regiments, Officers of the Guard and the Svodny Regiment. I was very happy to see my friend AKSHV in church, at breakfast and after that. [I] sat at Papa's table with Generals Maksimovich and Grishvald. The court orchestra played. In the afternoon Nastaska[41], Papa and I went for a walk, slid down the hill and

---

[39] Prayer service

[40] Count Alexander Vorontzov

[41] Sometimes Olga would refer to Anastasia with this nickname.

skated at the rink. It is snowing, but not so cold. Had tea with Papa and Mama. Poor Mama has a headache again and is not feeling well. We 4 went with Papa to the theater in Petersburg, to see "The Little Hunchback Horse" ballet. It was very nice. Saw Prince Beloselsky[42] with his son from far away. Returned [home] at 12 3/4. Mama was already in bed.

Olga with an officer

---

[42] Probably Prince Sergei Konstantinovich Belosselsky-Belozersky and his son Prince Sergei Sergeyevich.

Monday. 14 January. Had lessons. We 4 had breakfast at Mama's. She stayed in bed until tea as usual. Papa is at the German breakfast, because today is the German Emperor's birthday. Nastasia, Papa and I went for a walk. It is not that cold, but [there is] a blizzard. Had tea and dinner with Papa and Mama. Dear N.P. came over in the evening. [We] sat around cozily and talked. I felt so happy. Anya was here. Went to bed at about 10 1/2.

Tuesday. 15 January. Had lessons. Had breakfast with Papa, Aunt Olga and Uncle Petya[43]. Mama was lying down after breakfast. In the afternoon walked with Papa and Aunt Olga. It was 8 deg. below. Had tea with Papa, Mama, Aunt Olga and Uncle Petya. Then did homework. Had dinner with Mama and Anya. [We] spent the evening together too. Worked and talked. Papa went to the monthly Hussar Regiment [meeting]. Mama was tired. [We] talked a lot.

---

[43] Duke Peter of Oldenburg, Grand Duchess Olga Alexandrovna's first husband.

Olga with her aunt and namesake, "Aunt Olga" [Alexandrovna].

Wednesday. 16 January. Bekker[44] had arrived, this is why I stayed at home. Papa went to Petersburg for a reception and only returned for tea. We 4 had breakfast at Mama's. In the afternoon [I] sat with her and Anya – first in the bedroom, then in the study. Had dinner with Papa, Mama and Dmitri[45]. He was messing around with Papa. Then they went to play billiards, and we stayed with Mama.

---

[44] Olga is referring to her monthly period.

[45] Grand Duke Dmitri Pavlovich, the Tsar's first cousin - son of Grand Duke Pavel Alexandrovich.

Thursday. 17 January. Had lessons. Poor Mama still has a headache. This is the fourth week – May God help her. [We] sat with her in the afternoon, first in the bedroom, then in the parlor. Had tea with Papa, Mama, the sisters and Aleksei. T., Papa and I went to the opera – "Madame Butterfly". It was wonderful and sad. M.N. Kuznetsova[46] sang. Returned at about 12 o'cl. Mama was sitting with Anya.

Friday. 18 January. Had lessons. Had breakfast with Papa. In the afternoon Lili Obolenskaya and I rode in a sleigh. We steered the little chestnut horses ourselves [...]. They ran fast and really well. The weather is finally sunny and bright. After 4 o'cl. [we] sat in the parlor with Mama and Grigori Yefimovich[47]. We sat with Papa and Mama around him. It was very nice. We wore red blouses. We entered in the dark and so he thought we were wearing white. When the lights went on he was very surprised to see us dressed differently. He said: "The Lord allowed me see you in white when you came in because your souls are so pure". At the end Otetz Alexander Vas.[lievich] came over. [We] had dinner with Papa and Mama and went to bed early. Mama is still not feeling well and has a headache.

Saturday. 19 January. Had lessons as usual. 13 degrees below and brightly sunny in the morning. Had breakfast with Papa, Aunt Olga and Semyon Semyonovich. Mama had dinner with us, of course on the sofa. She does not

---

[46] Maria Nikolaevna Kuznetsova-Benois was one of the most celebrated opera singers in the imperial Russia.

[47] Grigori Yefimovich Rasputin.

seem to have a headache but is very tired. In the afternoon we 4 walked with

Papa and Aunt Olga. Walked around the pond. Had tea with them and Aleksei

and Mama. Went to vsenoshnaya at the regimental church. The Cossacks sang.

In the evening sat with Mama and Anya. Mama wore her new velvet cream

dress.

Sunday. 20 January. At 10 1/2 went to obednya at the regimental church. There

was a big breakfast and music. Sat with Baron Karf and Admiral Nilov[48] at Papa's

table. Saw my friend AKSHV, greeted him and felt happy, but did not talk to him.

At 2 o'cl. 7 min we 4 went to Petersburg with Olga Yevgenievna. Went to [see]

Grandmama at Anichkov and then went with Aunt Olga to her [house]. At 4 o'cl.

dear N.P., P.A. Voronov[49], S.S. Klyucharev, N.N. Rodionov, V.V. Kvoshinsky., A.

Shangin – a cuirassier and N.A. Kulikovsky[50] arrived. Aunt Olga was there. [We]

had tea and then ran around, played and danced to the phonograph until 6

o'clock. At 6 ½ [we] went to get dressed. Dinner was at 7 o'cl. 15 min. [I] sat with

Shangin and N.P. Was so happy to see him, the dear one, and talk to him. It

was sad not to see Mama for so long. She is still not feeling well, but is a little

better. At 8 o'cl. 45 min Papa came to get us and we went to the Mariinsky

Theater[51] with him to see the "Don Quixote" ballet. Pavlova[52] danced

---

[48] General-Adjutant Admiral Konstantin Dmitrievich Nilov was the Tsar's Flag Captain and one of his friends.

[49] Pavel Alekseyevich Voronov was an officer on The Standart and Olga's future love interest.

[50] Nikolai Alexandrovich Kulikovsky eventually became the second husband of Grand Duchess Olga Alexandrovna, the Tsar's sister.

[51] Imperial theater in St Petersburg.

[52] Anna Pavlova, the famous ballerina.

wonderfully. Saw Prince Beloselsky from afar. Returned at 12 o'cl. Anya was sitting with Mama.

Monday. 21 January. Had lessons. Had breakfast and dinner with Papa and Mama. Mama was lying down on the sofa and is feeling better, thank God. In the afternoon [I] walked with Papa. It is warmer but [there is] more snow. In the evening [we] sat with Mama and knitted. Papa read in his [room] and returned at 10 o'clock. After that we went to bed.

Tuesday. 22 January. Had lessons. 3 degrees below. At 10 o'cl. Otetz[53] Alexander came over and gave Mama communion. She is feeling better, thank God. Had breakfast with her and Trina[54]. Papa went to the consecration of the new barracks of the 4th Rifle Regiment's 2nd Battalion and had breakfast there. In the afternoon we 4 walked with him. There was more snow. Exercises at 4 o'cl. as usual. Uncle Pavel had tea with Papa and Mama. [We] had a dance lesson. Had dinner with Papa, Mama and Veselkin. Kaisorsky was telling funny stories. In the afternoon Lili Dehn[55] and Titi came to [see] Mama. So sweet.

Wednesday. 23 January. Had lessons. In the morning Mama went out on the balcony for the first time and is feeling better, thank God. Papa received 40 people in Petersburg and returned for tea. We 4 had breakfast with Mama, had

---

[53] Father/priest

[54] Catherine Schneider, one of the imperial tutors

[55] Julia "Lili" Dehn was the wife of an officer at court and Alexandra's friend. Titi was the nickname of her little son.

dinner with her and Papa. In the afternoon walked with Trina. Slid down the big hill on spades. There was more snow, it is warmer and slightly windy. Went to bed early.

Thursday. 24 January. Had lessons. Had breakfast with Papa and Mama. In the afternoon walked with Papa. It snowed the whole time. 1 1/2 degrees below. Mama sat on the balcony and is feeling better. At 4 o'cl. we 4 went to Petersburg with Papa. Stopped by Aunt Ksenia's, and then went to Grandmama's for tea and a Christmas party. Aunt Ksenia, Uncle Sandro[56] and the children, Aunt Olga and Uncle Petya [were there]. Got a lot of nice gifts. From there we went to Aunt Olga's for dinner. At 8.15 the little ones[57] went home with Trina, and we 2 and Papa went to the Alexandrinsky Theater – "The Assembly". Very interesting. Returned a little after midnight. Mama was in bed but not sleeping.

Friday. 25 January. Had lessons. Had breakfast with Mama. In the afternoon she went out on the balcony. She had a bit of a headache in the morning. Papa went to the Italian breakfast. In the afternoon we 4 slid down the big hill on spades. There was more snow and it is warm. Then Papa returned. Had dinner with Papa and Mama. Prayed with Aleksei.

---

[56] Grand Duke Alexander Mikailovich, Ksenia's husband.

[57] Meaning Maria and Anastasia and Aleksei.

"In the afternoon we 4 slid down the big hill on spades. There was more snow and it is warm."
Olga and Anastasia playing in the snow.

Saturday. 26 January. Had lessons. Had breakfast, tea and dinner with Papa, Mama and Aunt Olga. Mama is feeling better, thank God. She sat on the balcony for a half hour. In the afternoon we 4 walked with Papa and Aunt Olga. 1 degree below. Went to Vsenoshnaya at the regimental church. The Cossacks sang. In the evening sat with Mama, Papa and Aunt Olga. Went to sleep after 10 1/2.

Sunday. 27 January. At 10 ½ went to Obednya at the regimental church. The Cossacks sang. After that there was a big breakfast. Talked to the Svodny Regiment officers for a while. AKSHV was not there. I was angry. In the afternoon we 4 walked with Papa. Mama had a headache but she sat on the balcony anyway. Irina, Feodor, Rostislav[58], Vera and Georgi[59] had tea. Saw a cinematograph. Had dinner with Mama, Papa and Irina.

Monday. 28 January. Had lessons. Had breakfast with Mama. Papa went hunting, killed a lynx and 3 pheasants. In the afternoon we 4 slid down the hill on spades. Trina ran around with us. At 4 o'cl. 22 min Tatiana, Olga Yevgenievna and I went to Petersburg. We went directly to Anichkov [palace]. Grandmama hosted a Christmas party for the Cossacks, soldiers and officers. It was lots of fun. Talked to the guard officers. But my friend AKSHV was not there – [he] was sick. From there we went to Aunt Olga's for dinner. From there, [we] went to the circus with her and Irina. It was lots of fun. Dear N.P. was there. Returned and went to bed at about 12 o'cl.

Tuesday. 29 January. Had lessons. Had breakfast with Papa, Mama and N.P. In the afternoon skied down the hill with Papa. It was wonderful. Mama sat on the balcony in the afternoon. Aleksei played in the garden. Had dinner with Papa, Mama, N.P. and Anya. Spent the evening together until 10 1/2. Thank you, God. Save everyone.

---

[58] Olga's first cousins,daughter and sons of Grand Duchess Ksenia, the Tsar's sister.
[59] Youngest children of H.I.H. Grand Duke Konstantin Konstantinovich (KR)

Wednesday. 30 January. Had lessons. In the morning saw N.P. leaving in a troika[60] from the window. Papa went to Petersburg until tea. [We] had breakfast with Mama. After that we went out to the garden with Trina. Skied down the hill. It's cold but clear today, 10 degrees below. Mama went out on the balcony. In the evening we 2 and Papa went to the theater. Saw "The Legend of [Invisible City of] Kitezh" and " The Maiden Fevronia"[61]. Aunt Olga was there. It was very interesting and beautiful. Returned at about 12 o'clock.

Thursday. 31 January. Had lessons. Papa went to Petersburg for the viewing of Count Golenishev-Kutuzov's[62] body. After that he went to the Calvary Regiment. Had breakfast with Mama. She had a bit of a headache, but [still] went out on the balcony. In the afternoon we 4 went outside with Trina and skied down the hill. It was cold and clear. Had tea with Papa, Mama and Dmitri. Dinner with the same, and Uncle Pavel. Went to bed at 11 o'clock because Papa, Mama and Uncle Pavel were talking, and we 2 looked through [photo] albums with Dmitri and Papa in the large sitting room.

---

[60] Three horse sleigh or carriage.

[61] Opera in four acts by Nikolai Rimsly-Korsakov with a libretto by Vladimir Belsky

[62] Arseny Golenishev-Kutuzov was a famous Russian poet, and descendant of the famous general.

"..We[...] looked through albums..." Olga and her sisters were avid amateur photographers and loved to paste their pictures into albums.

~

February

Monday. 1 February. Had lessons as usual. Had breakfast and dinner with Papa, Mama and Sergei. Mama was lying on the sofa, because her heart is enlarged. In the afternoon Nastasia, Papa and I skied down the hill. It was not too cold and snowing. Had tea with Papa and Mama. Poor little Aleksei's arm hurts. He walked around for a bit with the doctor. Went to bed after 10. Thought a lot about yesterday.

Saturday. 2 February. Went to Obednya at the regiment [church] with Papa and Aunt Olga. Had tea, breakfast and dinner with Papa, Mama and Aunt Olga. In the afternoon went outside with Papa and Aunt and skied down the hill. Went to vsenoshnaya. In the afternoon Mama rode in a carriage with Anya, but got very tired in the evening, and heart No.2. In the evening went to Anya's. Mama, Papa, Lili Dehn with her husband, N.P., A.I. Butykov, S.V. Zlebov, N.P. Rodionov and L.M. Kozhevnikov were there. There was an English ventriloquist – very funny. After that we played dobchinsky-bobchinsky and then had dinner. Left at about 12 o'cl. Mama was very tired. I was so happy to see the dear sweet N.P.

Sunday. 3 February. Went to Obednya at 10 ½ , stayed in the chapel. Papa went to the 2nd Artillery Calvarly Regiment parade. Had breakfast with Mama. After that she played the piano for a while and sat on the balcony, but she is not feeling well because of yesterday. Skied down the hill with Papa. Cinematograph at 4 ½, Dmitri, Vasia and Rostislav came over. We 4 went the see the ballet "The Pharaoh's Daughter" with Papa. Pavlova danced. Aunt Olga was also there. Returned at about 1 in the morning. May the Lord save us.

Monday. 4 February. Had lessons. Had breakfast with Papa, Mama and Petrovsky. Mama sat at the table for the first time, went out on the balcony. In the afternoon [we] skied down the hill in the garden with Papa. The weather was wonderful – sunny and warm. Aleksei also came [with us]. Had dinner with Papa and Mama and went to bed early.

Tuesday. 5 February. Had lessons. Had breakfast and dinner with Papa, Mama and Kostya. At breakfast Mama sat at the table and then rode up the hill in a sled where we skied with Papa. Aleksei and Anya were there too. Sunny, warm, very nice. May the Lord save the angel-Mama. Went to bed at 10 o'cl. Papa read in his [room].

"... We skied with Papa."

Wednesday. 6 February. Had lessons. [It is] rather cold and windy. In the morning at 10 o'cl. 20 min Papa went to Petersburg for a reception. Had breakfast with Mama and R.A.Naryshkina. In the afternoon skied down the hill near the white tower with Anya. Papa returned after 3 o'clock and skied too. Mama did not go outside.

Thursday. 7 February. Had lessons. It is windy and rather cold, but sunny. Papa went to the Semyonovsky regiment and returned for tea. Had breakfast with

Mama and Anya. In the afternoon skied down the hill by the white tower. Mama did not go out. Had tea with her. Had dinner with her and Papa too. Before that Mama and Papa sat at Aleksei's upstairs. She had not been in his [room] for a long time. [We] sat with her in the evening. Papa read. Spoke on the telephone with Aunt Olga. Went to bed at 10 o'clock.

Friday. 8 February. Had lessons. About 8 degrees below. Had breakfast with Papa, Mama (she also sat)[63] and Uncle Georgi. In the afternoon skied down the hill by the white tower with Papa. Mama and Anya were there too. In the evening we 2 and Papa went to [see] an opera – Lohengrin: Sobinov, Golska, Cherkasskaya, etc. So beautiful – we saw it for the first time. Aunt Olga was there – the darling. Came home around 1 in the morning. Mama was tired.

Saturday. 9 February. Had lessons. Wonderful, sunny weather. Had breakfast with Papa, Mama and S.S. Poguliaev. Mama sat. Had dinner with the same, but Mama was lying down. In the afternoon skied down the hill near the white tower. Papa, Aunt Olga, the sisters, Anya and Sergei Sergeyevich P. were there, Mama and Aleksei too. It was lots of fun. Aunt Ksenia had tea. Went to vsenoshnaya.

Sunday. 10 February. Went to obednya at 10 ½. After that [we] had a big breakfast. At 2 o'cl. 7 min. we 4 and Olga Yevgenievna Byutzeva went to Petersburg to [see] Grandmama at Anichkov. After 3 o'cl. Aunt Olga took us to

---

[63] Possibly Olga mentioned this because Alexandra was usually lying down.

her [house]. Shangin came over there too. At about 3 ½ M.L. Tzigern-Shternberg and AKSHV came over there too and then – Skvortsov, Irina, Zoya, G. of Leuchtenberg[64] with Sasha and Nadya, N.N. Rodionov, V.V. Khvoshinsky, S.S. Klyucharev and N.A. Kulikovsky. [We] had tea, and then played in the large sitting room: cat and mouse, turkey, the ring, and also hide-and-seek downstairs in the dark. At dinner I sat with Tzigern-Shternberg and AKSHV. After that we went to the circus. Aunt Olga, K. Gagarin, Nadya, Klyucharev, Kulikovsky and 3 Cossacks. I sat with AKSHV the whole time and fell deeply in love with him. May the Lord keep us. Saw him all day long – at obednya and at breakfast, also in the afternoon and the evening. It was so nice and fun. He is so sweet. Came home with Lili Obolenskaya after 12 o'cl. Mama had a headache in the morning, and her heart was No.1-1/2. Aleksei's right arm hurts. Papa saw "Inspector General's Crooked Mirror" at the Chinese Theater. Thank you God for this day.

---

[64] Presumably this is George Maximilianovich, 6th Duke of Leuchtenberg

The two Olgas - aunt and niece - with officers. Officer on right appears to be Pavel Voronov.

Monday. 11 February. Had lessons as usual. Had breakfast and dinner with Papa, Mama and Sergei[65]. Mama was lying down on the sofa because her heart is enlarged. In the afternoon Nastasia, Papa and I skied down the hill. [It was] not too cold, and [was] snowing. Had tea with Papa and Mama. Poor little Aleksei's arm hurts. He walked around a bit with the doctor. Went to bed after 10 o'clock. Thought a lot about yesterday.

---

[65] Grand Duke Sergei Mikhailovich, one of the imperial cousins

Olga with her beloved little brother.

Tuesday. 12 February. In the morning it was 10 degrees below. Had lessons.

Had breakfast and tea with Papa, Mama, Uncle Petya, and darling Aunt Olga.

Skied down the hill with Nastaska. It was fun. Mama had No.2 in the morning,

and No.1 in the evening. She had a heart murmur. Aleksei is better, thank God,

but he did not get dressed and stayed downstairs. Had dinner with Papa, Mama

and Uncle Petya. In the evening Papa read to Mama. A delegation from my

regiment came to [see me]: Martynov, Gentselevich, Bekhterev and an unter-

officer. [...]

Wednesday. 13 February. Had lessons. Papa went to a reception in Petersburg. Mama does not feel well. Enlarged heart and tired. In the afternoon [we] skied down the hill with Nastasia. Papa returned at about 4 o'cl. and skied with us. Made us laugh. Had dinner with Papa and Mama. In the evening played kolorito with Mama. Went to bed at 10 o'cl. 5 min. Bekker came.

Thursday. 14 February. Stayed in bed all morning. Papa went to Petersburg. Had breakfast with Mama. After that rode in a sleigh with Maria and Trina. The weather is nice and sunny. Had tea with Papa and Mama. Dinner with the same, and also Sashka. The little ones watched a cinematograph.

Friday. 15 February. Had lessons. Had breakfast with Mama. Papa was with the Emir of Bukhara, who brought wonderful gifts for all. Tried them on in the afternoon, and that's why poor Mama got very tired. Rode with Lili Ob[olenskaya]. Cold. Stayed downstairs with Mama until tea in the large sitting room. Everyone sat together with Grigori Yefimovich. Papa was also there of course. He[66] kept patting Aleksei's head and said that I could rule like the tsarinas did in the past. Had dinner with Papa and Mama.

Saturday. 16 February. Had lessons. Aunt Ella[67] arrived. Had breakfast, tea and dinner with her, Papa, Mama and Aunt Olga. Rode with Lili Ob[olenskaya]. Very

---

[66] Rasputin

[67] Grand Duchess Elisaveta Feodorovna, Alexandra's sister.

cold. Mama has a headache and is not feeling well. Went to vsenoshnaya at the regimental church. In the evening watched a cinematograph "The Election of Tsar Mikhail"[68], etc. Very interesting. Went to bed at 12 ½.

Olga (center) with her parents, sisters and "Aunt Ella" in her nun's habit.

Sunday. 17 February. At 10 ½ went to obednya. After that had breakfast with Papa, Mama, Ioann[69] and Aunt Ella. The Pochaevsky Icon of Theotokos[70]

---

[68] Tsar Mikhail was the first tsar of the Romanov dynasty.

arrived in the afternoon. An obednitza[71] was held. At 2 o'cl. 7 min. we 4 with Lili

Ob[olenskaya] went to Petersburg to [see] Grandmama at Anichkov [palace].

From there [we] went with Aunt Olga to her [house]. At 3 1/2 M. L. Tsigern-

Shternberg, A.S. Fedyushkin and dear AKSHV [arrived]. [We] sat around cozily,

and did not talk much, were mostly quiet. Around 4 o'clock the rest arrived: Count

Leuchtenberg with Sasha, Kolya and Nadya, Zoya, Irina, N.N. Rodionov, S.S.

Klyucharev, R. Shangin and N.A. Kulikovsky [all] came over. Had tea at 2 tables.

I sat with AKSHV. He was wearing a dark-colored cherkeska[72] but not his military

jacket. He is so sweet. I was very, very happy. After that we played various

games in the parlor and hide-and-seek downstairs. It was lots and lots of fun. Left

at 7 o'cl., very sad. Looked at him through the window when they were leaving.

Had dinner with the same as breakfast. At 9 o'cl. we 2 went to the town hall with

Papa to see the amateur play "The Eternal Love", which benefitted the Red

Cross. Olya [?illegible] was performing. A lot of acquaintances were there. The

play ended exactly at midnight. Mama was already in bed, very tired. Poor Angel

– may God save her.

Monday. 18 February. Had lessons. In the morning it was 14 degrees below,

sunny. Had breakfast with Mama and Aunt Ella. Papa was at the Grand Palace

with the Khan of Khiva. In the afternoon we 4 skied down the hill. Had tea with

---

[69] Prince Ioann Konstantinovich, son of Grand Duke Konstantin Konstatinovich (KR).

[70] Icon of the Mother of God from The Pochaev monastery.

[71] Liturgy without communion performed without a priest, or where a deacon has been permittied to serve communion by a bishop

[72] A type of overcoat

Papa, Mama and Aunt Ella. Had dinner with the same, and also Uncle Pavel. Mama's heart is No.2 and she is tired.

Tuesday. 19 February. Had lessons. It is windy, and the snow seems to be melting. Had breakfast, tea and dinner with Papa, Mama and Aunt Ella. In the afternoon sat with Mama. Her heart is No.2, and she is very tired. At 4 o'clock went to Petersburg directly to the Cathedral of Christ the Savior for obednitza. Grigori Yefimovich was there. In the evening darling Aunt Olga came over. [We] sat together and worked. Listened on the telephone. T. and I are [staying] in the same room – cozy. May the Lord save us.

"T. and I are [staying] in the same room – cozy."

Wednesday. 20 February. In the morning we 4 rode in a sleigh with Trina. Went down Nevsky, Morskoy, the waterfront, where we saw the dear Standart up close. Before breakfast saw dear N.P. with Rodionov, [they] were walking along the waterfront. Had breakfast with Papa, Aunt Ella and Dmitri. Mama was lying down on her sofa. She was tired, the poor angel. In the afternoon we 2 went to St Peter and Paul Fortress with Papa for a molebna. Papa wore [his] Yerivansky regiment uniform. There were masses of people. Saw Count Nirod[73], Prince B.[eloselsky]-B.[elozersky] from far away. After we returned we sat with Mama, Aunt Ksenia and Grandmama. Had tea with Papa, Mama and Aunt Olga. Had dinner with Mama and Aunt Ella. Spent the evening all together. Papa was at Grandmama's at Anichkov.

---

[73] Count M.E. Nirod was one of the imperial attendants. The more common English spelling is "Nieroth", but I will use the transliterated version here.

Olga, "Mama" and "Papa" with the suite

Thursday. 21 February[74]. Walked in the garden. Sunny, warm, muddy and windy. At 12 o'cl. 15 min. went to the Kazan Cathedral for molebna. Papa and Aleksei rode in a carriage with a hundred escort guards at the front. Saw **AKSHV** from very far away. Then Mama and Grandmama [rode] in a carriage, then we 4 and another hundred escort guards. In the Cathedral and at the reception [I] saw dear N.P., Prince B.-B. and Count Nirod. Had breakfast with Grandmama, Papa and Aunt Ella. Mama was in her [room] on the **sofa**. At 3 o'cl. 45 min. went to the reception wearing Russian dresses. Tatiana and I have not worn these dresses

---

[74] 21 February (Old Style) was the commemoration of the assumption of the throne by Tsar Mikhail Romanov. This ceremony marked the official start of the Tercentenary celebrations of the House of Romanov.

before. Mama was wearing a cloth of gold dress. She of course felt very tired, poor angel. It ended at 5 1/2 . Had dinner with Papa and Aunt Ella. She left in the evening. Sat with Mama.

"...Went to the reception wearing Russian dresses". Olga in a traditional Russian court dress.

Friday. 22 February. There was a reception at 11 o'clock. All the relatives were there. Mama was not there – heart No.2. Had breakfast with Papa, Grandmama, Aunt Olga, Aunt Ksenia and Uncle Petya. In the afternoon walked in the garden with Papa. Had tea with Papa, Mama and Grandmama. After that there was a reception for diplomats, but we were not there – poor Tatiana is in bed with fever. In the evening [we] watched the folk play "Life for the Tsar"[75]. Very beautiful and festive. Mama left after the first act because she was not feeling well at all and was tired. Saw N.P., Prince B.-B. with his wife, Count Nirod[76] with his wife, etc. Returned home at 11 1/2. – The whole city was celebrating, masses of people. Thank God that everything is well. In the afternoon talked to N.P. on the telephone.

Saturday. 23 February. In the morning walked in the garden with Papa. Warm. Went to a reception for the ladies-in-waiting with Grandmama. Had breakfast with Papa and Grandmama. Mama does not feel well at all, hence [she] is lying down. In the afternoon Irina, the boys and I sat with Tatiana. She still has fever and is in bed. Had dinner with Papa. At 9 o'cl. 15 min went to the Assembly of the Nobility with Papa and Mama. Prayers were chanted, speeches made, and bread-and-salt served. After the polonaise, [I] walked with Count Sievers. After that the dancing started. I danced a lot - it was such fun. Masses of people. Saw N.P. (with whom I spoke on the telephone in the afternoon), his brother, Prince B.-B. and lots of other friends. Mama left in the middle [of it]. We and Papa left at 11

---

[75] "A Life for the Tsar" - an Opera in four acts by Mikhail Glinka (cr. 1836)

[76] Count M. E. Nirod was one of the imperial attendants.

o'cl. 45 min. It was so beautiful. I danced a quadrille with Zinoviev, mazurka – with Oleg K., and other dances with lots of officers. My first ball.

"We 3" Olga with Tatiana and Maria

Sunday. 24 February. Went to obednya. Before that all the clergy processed with icons before Papa. We 3 had breakfast with him. Poor Tatiana has fever of 39.2 and a headache. It's very sad that she cannot go anywhere. At 2 o'cl. we 3 and Aunt Olga went to her [house]. Tzigern-Shternberg, Skvortsov and dear AKSHV [who was wearing] a dark-colored cherkesska[77] also went there. Then dear N.P., Klyucharev, G. of **Leuchtenberg** with Sasha, Nadya and Kolya, Irina, Zoya,

---

[77] The full-skirted Caucasian-style coat which is the chief part of the Cossack uniform

Nikolasha Zarnikau, Shangin and Kulikovsky came over. In the spare dining hall [we] played turkey, all-of-Petersburg, slap-on-hands, but most of all rope. It was so wonderful – unbelievable. At tea I sat between N.P. and **AKSHV** and felt incredibly happy. Saw them together for the first time. Spoke to Mama on the telephone. She stayed in bed all day because she was not feeling well. After tea [we] played hide-and-seek downstairs in the dark, then played upstairs again. Returned at about 6, got dressed and went to Mama's. Together we went to the Malachite Room to join the [rest of] the family. From there Mama walked to dinner in the Georgievsky Hall arm-in-arm with D. Nikitin. Verkhovsky, Count Nirod, Grigori and [illeg.] were standing behind me. There was music and masses of people. Mama was tired and spent the evening on the **sofa**. Anya was there. In the afternoon Papa visited the People's House. Went to bed at 10 1/2. Thank you Lord for everything. May the Lord keep everyone.

The code Olga used in her diary to refer to her love interest "AKSHV"

Monday. 25 February. Spent the morning with Mama, near her bed. Her heart is enlarged. Went to church at 11 1/2 and at 7 o'cl. Had breakfast with Papa, K.D. Tatanov and Boris[78] and K. Bagration[79]. In the afternoon we 3 and Papa walked

---

[78] Grand Duke Boris Vladimirovich, son of Grand Duke Vladimir and Maria Pavlovna the Elder.

on the roof, and then in the garden. It was windy. Poor Tatiana still has fever [of] 39.4, but her headache is not as bad. Grandmama and Aunt Ksenia came over to see her. Had tea with Mama and Anya. Papa was at Aunt Miechen's[80]. Had dinner with them and Bagration. Darling Aunt Olga came over in the evening. She, Mama, Papa and I watched M[aria] and A[nastasia] swim in Papa's big bathtub – [it was] very funny. After that we sat and worked. Mama's heart [is] No.2. Went to bed at about 11 o'cl.

Tuesday. 26 February. Went to church. Then had breakfast with Papa and Uncle Pavel. In the morning Tatiana had fever 39.1, in the evening – 39.6. At 2 o'cl. [we] went to the Fortress to visit Grandpapa's grave, then to the panikhida[81]. Returned from there with Grandmama, Aunt Olga, Aunt Ksenia and Uncle Sandro. Bid farewells and went to Tsarskoe Selo. Had tea with Papa and Mama. Mama does not feel well. Went to church.

Wednesday. 27 February. Had lessons and went to church. Mama does not feel well. Yesterday's trip bent her out of shape. Tatiana had fever in the morning and in the evening, 39.7. I went to see her a few times. Had breakfast with Papa, Mama and Zhitkevich. Built a [snow] tower near the ice rink with Papa. Aleksei rode there in a carriage. The weather is sunny and wonderful, blue sky. Had tea

---

[79] Prince Konstantin Bagration-Moukhransky – a Russian nobleman and member of the former Georgian Royal family.

[80] Grand Duchess Maria Pavlovna the Elder, wife of Grand Duke Vladimir, an imperial cousin.

[81] Annual memorial service for the deceased Emperor Alexander III

and breakfast with Papa and Mama. In the evening sat at Mama's with Anya. Papa read.

Thursday. 28 February. Had lessons. Went to church. Had breakfast and dinner with Papa, Mama and Count Grabbe[82]. Tatiana's [temperature] was 39.1 in the morning, and 38.4 in the evening, she took a bath. In the afternoon [we] built the tower on the ice rink with Papa. Warm. Had tea with Papa and Mama. Went to church. Mama and Aleksei went too. Went to bed after 10 o'clock.

"In the afternoon [we] built the tower on the ice rink with Papa."

~

---

[82] General Count Alexander Grabbe

March

Friday. 1 March. We 3 and the music teacher rode in a sleigh. It was sunny, 3 degrees in the afternoon, warm. Tatiana's [temperature] was 38.1 in the morning, in the afternoon 37.8, 38.6 in the evening. She is feeling better. We 3 with Papa and N.P. were building the tower on the ice rink. Aleksei was also there. Had breakfast and dinner with Papa, Mama and the dear, dear N.P. Had tea with Papa and Mama. Went to church in the morning and in the evening. Mama went too. She was in a cheerful mood, thank God. At 10 o'cl. Mama and Papa confessed in the bedroom. Thank you God for this day.

Olga with "Mama"

Saturday. 2 March. Went to obednya at 9 o'cl. Received communion. In the afternoon the Batushka[83] brought the Eucharist to Tatiana upstairs and gave her communion. In the morning [her temperature]: 38.1, 38.7, 38.9, she is tired. Sweet dear N.P. was at church. Later had tea with Papa and Mama. Had breakfast at 1 o'clock with them and Count Fredericks[84]. Aunt Olga arrived around 2 o'clock. Worked with her and Papa [breaking] the ice for a while. It was raining, everything was thawing, and the ice was cracking. The tower is heavy.

[83] Priest, literally "Little Father"
[84] Count Vladimir Fredericks was the imperial household minister

Then we walked around the garden. Mary[85] pushed Aleksei around in a wheelchair. Had tea and dinner with Mama and Aunt Olga. Finally went to vsenoshnaya at the regimental church. In the evening sat with Mama and Anya. Papa read in his [room].

Olga with "sweet dear N.P.[Sablin]"

Sunday. 3 March. Papa went to Prince N. Dolgoruky's[86] funeral in Petersburg. [We] went to obednya at the regimental church. Had breakfast with Mama and Anya. Her heart is No.1, and she was tired ever since Petersburg. Tatiana's

[85] Maria Ivanovna Vishnyakova, one of the children's nannies.

[86] [86] Prince Nikolai Sergeievich Dolgorukov (1840-1913), Court Chamberlain of Alexander II

[temperature] in the morning [was] 38.3, 39, after bath – 38.9. In the afternoon [we] went out to the garden with Papa. The water is ankle deep around the tower, and even deeper in some places. Aleksei will have 4 boys over. Aunt Ksenia, Georgi, Vera are with M[aria] and A[nastasia]. I feel lonesome, did not see AKSHV today. It rained and snowed, [but was] warm. Had tea with Papa and Mama. Went to bed at 10 o'clock.

Monday. 4 March. Had lessons. Had breakfast and dinner with Papa and Mama. Tatiana's temperature: 38.1, 37.5, 38.4. in the afternoon went to [see] the recruits of the 1st and the 2nd Mine Division and Underwater Navigation. They had excellent maneuvers. In the evening sat with Mama. [It was] sunny, a little windy.

Tuesday. 5 March. Had lessons. Had breakfast and dinner with Papa and the Frenchman, had dinner at the Hussar regiment. Aunt Olga was here from 2 until 7 o'clock. Sat with her and Mama at T[atiana]'s, who had her hair cut short. In the morning [her temperature was]: 38.9, 39.1, after bath – 39. Papa walked with Aunt Olga, but we did not [go] because of runny noses. In the evening sat with Mama and Anya.

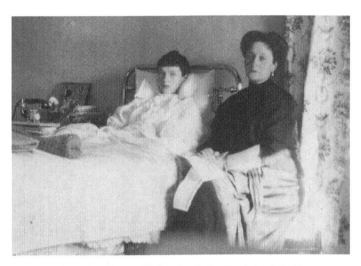

"Sat with... Mama at T[atiana]'s, who had her hair cut short."

Wednesday. 6 March. Had lessons. In the morning sat with T. : [crossed out],

37.7, 38.5. Had breakfast and dinner with Papa, Mama and Sem.[yon]

Sem.[yonovich]. In the afternoon Mama and Papa went to Grandmama's in

Petersburg. Her brother, the King of Greece[87] was killed yesterday in Saloniki. In

the evening sat with Mama, the trip tired her out. Snow, warm, sunny and windy.

Thursday. 7 March. Had lessons. Had breakfast, tea and dinner with Papa and

Mama. Warm and sunny. In the afternoon walked in the garden with Papa, then

had a snowball fight with Aunt Ksenia's boys on ice. Mama's heart was over 3 in

the morning, and 2 in the evening, she was very tired. T's temperature: 37.6 in

---

[87] King George I of Greece was fatally shot by an alleged member of a socialist group.

the morning, 38, 38.9, after bath – 39.1. We 3 went to the regimental church, inside the cathedral and stayed there for 10 minutes, and walked around the church for ¼ of an hour, because the doors were locked.

Friday. 8 March. Had lessons. T: in the morning – 37.1, 38, 38.2. Mama's heart is enlarged, she does not feel well. Had breakfast with Papa and Mama. In the afternoon we 3 took a walk, scraped the ice with [our] feet. Had dinner with Mama and sat with her until 10 o'cl. Played kolorito[88] 3 times and worked. Papa was in Petersburg at Grandmama's.

Saturday. 9 March. Had lessons. Had breakfast with Papa, Aunt Olga, Count Fredericks and darling Count Nirod. Mama was on her sofa, did not feel well. T's temperature in the morning [was] 36.9, 37.1, 37.9. Thank God everyone is well. Now poor Evgeny Sergeyevich Botkin[89] is sick, probably also typhoid. In the afternoon walked with Papa and Aunt Olga. Had tea with them and Mama. Went to vsenoshnaya at the regimental church. Went to bed at 10 1/2 . Sat with Mama and Anya. Papa read.

Sunday. 10 March. Went to obednya at the regimental church with Papa. Yesterday and today I wore black for the first time. Had breakfast with Papa, Mama and Knyazhevich. Tatiana's temperature in the morning 36.5, 36.3, 37.6. She is cheerful. At 2 o'cl. 7 min we 3 went to Petersburg with Olga

---

[88] A game

[89] One of the imperial physicians.

Yevg[enievna], to Grandmama's at Anichkov. Aunt Ksenia, Aunt Olga and Irina were there. Then poor Aunt Minnie[90] arrived. We stayed there for a while, then went to Aunt Olga's. Had tea with her, looked at her albums. Papa received Mr. Franklin. We also went to her exhibit in the hall. All [from] the students of Krisitsky. It was wonderful to be with the darling Aunt, of course, but I was sad without AKSHV. Returned at 6 1/2. Had dinner with Papa and Mama. In the evening played kolorito with Mama. Her heart was not well and because of that her temperature was 37.2. May God save her. Rode with Aunt Olga along Morskaya [Street] and saw the dear beloved yacht up close.

Olga wearing what appears to be mourning black

---

[90] Princess Maria of Greece and Denmark , daughter of King George I of Greece and Grand Duchess Olga Konstantinovna

Monday. 11 March. Thick fog. Had lessons. Tatiana's temperature in the morning 36.6, 36.6, 36.9. Had breakfast and dinner with Papa and Mama. In the morning went to see the Revel recruits parade. The dear N.P. was there. Sirotinin came to see Mama in the morning. Her heart is not well. Botkin is very ill. In the evening Papa told us about the winter house at Gatchina. It was so cozy.

Tuesday. 12 March. Had lessons. Anastasia's leg hurts and she was lying down. T[atiana]'s temperature was normal - 37 in the afternoon. Had breakfast with Papa and Mama. 3 degrees. In the afternoon Papa and I broke the ice for the first time. It was fun. Mama has a bad headache and is not feeling well. In the evening [I] played kolorito with her. She felt better and more energetic. Papa read in his [room]. Went to bed at 10 o'cl.

"In the afternoon Papa and I broke the ice for the first time."

Wednesday. 13 March. Had lessons. The weather is wonderful. 13 degrees. Around 5 [degrees], higher than 10 in the sun. Papa went to a reception in Petersburg. Had breakfast with Mama. In the afternoon walked with Trina. Delcroix washed all of our hair with kerosene[91], and now [our] hair is awfully dry and sticking out all over. T[atiana]'s temperature is normal. Nastasia is still in bed. Had dinner with Papa and Mama. In the evening [I] went to another part of

---

[91] This was one of 19th-early 20th century remedies for head lice

the house to choose vases for the bazaar[92], etc. Mama slept for only 2 hours today and is not feeling well. She felt a bit better in the evening.

Thursday. 14 March. Had lessons. Had breakfast, tea and dinner with Papa and Mama. In the afternoon rode with Trina. It is 18 degrees in the sun but windy. Tatiana is feeling well, she ate a piece of prosphora[93] and a piece of toast. Mama did not sleep well, her heart is still enlarged and she is tired. Papa had a Historical Society meeting at 9 o'cl.

Friday. 15 March. Had lessons. Had breakfast and dinner with Papa and Mama. In the afternoon rode with Anastasia and Nastenka. It was 10 [degrees] in the sun, but 0 in the shade. Aunt Ksenia and Uncle Sandro had tea with Papa and Mama. T[atiana] is fine. Mama played kolorito 3 times in the evening. She felt better in the evening. Papa read.

Saturday. 16 March. Had lessons. It is colder today, but very warm in the sun. Had breakfast with Papa, Mama, Aunt Olga, Gavril[94] and Fredericks. In the afternoon [I] rode with Nastasia and Aunt Olga. It was very nice. Had tea with Papa, Mama and Aunt Olga. Had dinner with the same and Gavril. Went to vsenoshnaya.

---

[92] Charity bazaar in Yalta, Crimea.

[93] Prosphora is bread which has been blessed on the altar during the liturgy. In the Russian Orthodox tradition, it is distributed at the end of the service, and is often taken home to the sick, or to those who could not attend Holy Communion.

[94] H.H. Prince Gavril Konstantinovich of Russia, son of Grand Duke Konstantin Konstantinovich (KR).

Sunday. 17 March. Went to obednya. Otetz Shavelsky performed the service yesterday and today. Had breakfast with Papa, Mama, Ioann and Gavril. At 2 o'cl. 7 min we 4 went to Petersburg to Grandmama's with them and Lili Obolenskaya. Aunt Olga and Aunt Ksenia were there. Aunt Ksenia is leaving for Paris today. A little after 3 o'clock [we] went to Aunt Olga's with her. At 3 1/2 Tzigern-Shternberg, Gozeko, Skvortsov and AKSHV arrived. Dear, sweet AKSHV, I was so happy to finally see him. Prince Leuchtenberg with Irina, Fedor and Andrusha[95] had tea. We had tea with the same on the little balcony in the sun. It was so cozy. We sat and talked for a long while. Then [we] went to play turkey, rope, and slap-on-hands in the spare dining room. Had dinner at 6 1/2 . We 3 and Aunt Olga sat with the Cossacks at their table. I also sat with AKSHV at tea. We walked around, sat, talked and laughed until 8 o'cl., it was so nice. Poor darling, he told me that his mother died last year. I am so sad for him. May the Lord save us. Returned at 8 o'cl. 15 min with Olga Yevg[enievna]. In the evening sat with Papa and Mama. Stopped by Tatiana's [room], she is feeling fine. This afternoon Mama rode in an equipage and felt a bit queasy and tired. Darling Aunt Olga took 2 photographs of us three with the Cossacks. Kulikovsky and Shangin were also there.

---

[95] Fedor and "Andrusha" (Andrei) were sons of Grand Duchess Ksenia, and Irina Alexandrovna's brothers, i.e. Olga's first cousins.

Olga, Maria and Anastasia with their "darling Aunt Olga"

Monday. 18 March. Had lessons. Had breakfast and dinner with Papa, Mama and Kostya. In the afternoon went to review the 1st Baltic Navy Crew. It was very nice. 18 degrees in the sun, so warm. N.P. and a few other officers from the yacht were there. T. is fine. Now Trina is sick. Aleksei stayed in bed. In the evening Papa read reports by K. Ad. Petrov from Sevastopol and by K. Gr. Vorozheikin from "The Russia" [...]. Mama and I worked.

Tuesday. 19 March. Had lessons. Nice weather - 21 [degrees] in the sun, over 5 in the shade, and the air is warm and spring-like. Had breakfast, tea and dinner with Papa, Mama and Dmitri. In the afternoon broke the ice with him, the sisters, Aleksei, Mary, R.P. Derevenko and Papa. It was so nice. T. was lying down on the sofa and walking around for a bit. In the evening played kolorito with Mama. She is feeling a bit better. Papa played billiards with Dmitri. Went to vsenoshnaya at the lower church[96] – cozy.

Wednesday. 20 March. At 10 o'cl. 25 min. Papa and I went to the Greek church in Petersburg to the panikhida[97] for Uncle Willy[98]. Antiochian Patriarch Grigori performed the service. N.P. was there. I was happy to see him. Went to Grandmama's for breakfast. Dear Aunt Olga was there. After we returned, we got busy breaking the ice. 11 [degrees] in the shade and 22 in the sun – wonderful weather. Had dinner with Papa. Poor Mama has a severe headache.

Thursday. 21 March. Had lessons. Had breakfast and dinner with Papa and Mama. In the afternoon broke the ice with Papa and smoked in the garden. It was 23 in the sun and over 10 in the shade. So nice. Had tea with Papa, Mama and Irina. T. came downstairs for the first time today. Went to vsenoshnaya at the lower church. Mama's headache is better, but [her] heart is enlarged.

---

[96] The "Lower Church" refers to the private chapel of the Imperial Family in the lower level of the Feodorovsky Cathedral

[97] Prayer service for the deceased

[98] King George I of Greece's nickname was "Uncle Willy", who was assassinated on 18th March, 1913.

"… Smoked in the garden." The grand duchesses smoking a cigarette. All the girls smoked, as well as their parents.

Friday. 22 March. At 9 o'cl. 45 min. we 3 went to Petersburg with Papa to the Second All-Russian Craft Exhibition. Stayed there for 2 hours, walked around, looked at everything. Everything was interesting. Had breakfast at Grandmama's with Uncle Petya, Aunt Olga and Irina, who also went to the exhibition. After we returned, broke the ice with Papa in the garden. 8 degrees in the shade. It was foggy in the morning. Had dinner with Papa, Mama and Dmitri. In the evening played kolorito with Mama. She is not feeling well. [Our] brother, T., Mikhail, Pavel had tea with them. T came downstairs and had dinner. Went to bed at 10 o'cl.

Olga, Tatiana, Aleksei and their parents with Grand Duke Dmitri

Saturday. 23 March. Had lessons. Had breakfast and dinner with Papa, Mama, Aunt Olga and Veselkin, who told a lot of funny jokes. T. was downstairs the entire time, and is much more cheerful. She got a lot taller. In the afternoon walked with Papa and Aunt Olga. Then broke the ice. 4 [degrees] in the shade, and chilly, I think. Had tea with Papa, Mama and Aunt Olga. Went to vsenoshnaya. The regimental choir sang, and Otetz Andreyev performed the service because it was the regiment holiday. In the evening sat with Mama – she does not feel well.

Sunday. 24 March. Went to obednya. Ioann R.'s choir sang. In the evening the entire imperial court went to vsenoshnaya. There was a big breakfast. Dear AKSHV was there, and also at the church. In the afternoon we broke the ice with Papa and Irina. 5 degrees. Had tea with Irina, Papa and Mama. T was also there. Had dinner with Papa, Mama and Prince Bagration. In the evening N.P. and Anya came over. Papa read in his [room]. Mama is not feeling well. It was cozy.

Monday. 25 March. At 10. 25 we 3 and Papa went to Petersburg. Maria and Nastasia went to Grandmama's at Anichkov for obednya. Papa and I went to see the Calvalry regiment parade. It was very beautiful. Saw N.P. and B.-B. From there went to Grandmama's for breakfast with Aunt Olga. Aunt Ksenia and her daughter[99] were there. At 2 o'cl. 15 min went with Aunt Olga to her [house]. At about 3 o'cl. AKSHV, Yuzik, Skvortsov and V.E. Zborovsky arrived there. We all sat together for a long time, and it was awkward at first. Had tea in the sitting room on the little balcony. I sat on the sofa between AKSHV and Skvortsov. Then T. of Leuchtenberg, Sasha, Kolya, Irina, Andrusha, Fedor, Shangin, Nikolasha,

---

[99] H.H. Princess Irina Alexandrovna of Russia, later Princess Yusupov, Countess Soumarokoff-Elston.

Kulikovsky and later Tsengern-Shternberg arrived. Played turkey and rope for a long while in the spare dining room. It was such fun. At dinner I sat with Tsengern and again with dear sweet AKSHV. He wore a light grey cherkesska and a black beshmet[100] as usual. He was awfully sweet, talkative and cheerful. After that we went to the Aunt's study, sat there and talked and laughed. At 8 o'cl. 15 min. [we] left with Nastenka[101]. It was so nice. Papa went to a concert [performed] by invalids. Mama was lying down and Anya was there with her. Mama is not feeling well, her heart is enlarged.

---

[100] Overcoat with no buttons

[101] Anastasia Hendrikova, lady at court and Olga's friend.

Tatiana, Nicholas, Anastasia and Olga taking a walk. Maria is behind Nicholas

Tuesday. 26 March. Had lessons. Had breakfast with Papa and Sergei. Mama did not get up all day by Sirotinin's[102] orders. Her heart is not well, and that causes [her] temperature to go up to 37. In the afternoon we broke the ice with Papa. Maria slipped into water. But it was a lot of fun. The sun came out and it

---

[102] One of the imperial physicians

got brighter. Only 1 degree and cloudy. In the evening played kolorito[103] with Mama. Spoke on the telephone with Anya, Lili Dehn, Rodionov and Voronov. Thought about yesterday.

Wednesday. 27 March. Had lessons. We 3 had breakfast by ourselves. Papa went to the Dragoon celebration. He had dinner with the 1st Infantry Regiment. In the afternoon we broke the ice with him. Sunny, 4 [degrees] in the shade. T came out on the balcony for 45 minutes. Went to vsenoshnaya at the lower church. After dinner sat with Mama on her bed. She only got up for tea today. She does not feel well. Anya came over.

Thursday. 28 March. After lessons at 11 o'cl. went to the manege[104] for moleben and parade of the Svodny Regiment with Papa and Aunt Olga, which was rescheduled from 23 March. Marie, Loman[105], M. Loman, Sherekhovsky, Khailov, Kutepov, M. Krestianova and M. Andreyeva sat at my table. Music was playing. Walked and broke the ice in the afternoon. [It] rained and snowed. Had tea with Papa, Mama and Irina. Aunt Olga left. Had dinner with the sisters upstairs. Papa went to [see] the regiment, Mama was in bed. She is a little better today. Played kolorito with her 3 times. Anya was here.

---

[103] A board game (cr. 1892) similar to checkers which was a favorite of the Imperial Family.

[104] Riding hall

[105] Colonel Dmitri Nikolaevich Loman, of Svodny Infantry Regiment

Friday. 29 March. Had lessons. Had breakfast and dinner with Papa and Uncle Petya. Mama was in bed and only got up for tea, same as yesterday. In the afternoon broke the ice with Papa. It snowed in the morning. 2 degrees in the afternoon, damp and foggy. After dinner played kolorito with Mama.

Saturday. 30 March. Had lessons. Had breakfast with Papa, Aunt Olga, Uncle Mitya and Mordvinov. Mama stayed in her bedroom. In the afternoon walked and broke the ice with Papa and Aunt Olga. It was sunny, then rained, then cleared up, then cloudy. 3 degrees. Had tea with the same and Mama. Had dinner with the same and also Dmitri. Mama stayed in her [room]. Played kolorito with her. Went to vsenoshnaya at the regimental church.

Sunday. 31 March. Went to obednya at the regimental church. The Cossacks sang very well. After that there was a big breakfast. Prince B.-B. and AKSHV were there. At 2 o'cl. 7 min. we 3 with Lili Ob[olenskaya] went to Petersburg. The same ones who had breakfast with us also went there but later by train. Grandmama and Aunt Olga played bezique[106]. At 3 o'cl. 5 min. [we] went to Aunt Olga's. AKSHV, Yuzik, Skvortsov and Zablodsky were already there. Sat all together. Aunt took our picture and at 4 o'cl we went to have tea on the little balcony. As usual, [I] sat on the sofa with AKSHV and Skvortsov on [my] other side. It was nice and cozy. He was wearing a light gray cherkesska and a beautiful beshmet. So sweet and nice. Irina with [her] 2 brothers, T. Leuchtenberg with Sasha and Kolya, Klyucharev and Shangin arrived. We

---

[106] A card game

played falcon, cat-and-mouse, turkey, rope, slap on the hands, etc. in the hall. Towards the end Tzengern-Shternberg, Kulikovsky, Leuchtenberg, D. Kalinin, Itashev, and Plevitskaya came over, [and] stayed for dinner. The last one to arrive was Felix[107], so awfully civilian that the Cossacks wanted to beat him up. Left at 7 o'cl. 15 min. Did not want to leave them. Had dinner with Papa and played kolorito with Mama later in the evening. She was on the sofa and feeling better, thank God.

"The last one to arrive was Felix, so awfully civilian that the Cossacks wanted to beat him up."
Felix Yusupov is on the right.

---

[107] Prince Felix Yussupov, the future husband of Olga's cousin Irina.

April

Monday. 1 April. Had lessons. Had breakfast with Papa, Mama and Aunt Olga. At 2 ½ went to the ceremonial review of guard recruits, Infantry school and the Baltic Naval Crew. Sports exercises, regimental exercises and ceremonial marching, very nice. The weather was foul, [it] snowed the entire time. Saw AKSHV briefly from far away. N.P. and other yacht officers were there. Had dinner with Papa, Mama and Daragan[108]. In the evening Papa read. I played kolorito with Mama. She is better but looks pale.

Tuesday. 2 April. Had lessons. Had breakfast with Papa, Mama, M. and Uncle Sergei. In the afternoon broke the ice with Papa. [There was] a lot of snow and chilly. At 8 o'clock M, Papa and I went to Petersburg to a concert at the Mariinsky Theater. V.V. Andreyev's 25th anniversary. The balalaika players were wonderful. N.V. Plevitskaya sang. The tributes were long and boring. But dear N.P. was there, as well as Aunt Olga. Returned at 12 ½.

Wednesday. 3 April. Had lessons. Had breakfast with Papa, Mama and N.P. Had dinner with the same and Anya. T rode in the garden for the first time, and ate with us too. In the afternoon Papa and N.P. broke the ice. It was so nice to be with him, the dear one. It was chilly. Watched the 2nd Infantry regiment practice. I

---

[108] Fligel Adjutant/Colonel Daragan

was very happy to see him. Mama was on the balcony for ¼ of an hour. I went to bed at 10 o'cl. while Papa, Mama, N.P. and Anya started to play kosti[109].

Thursday. 4 April. Had lessons. Had breakfast with Papa, Mama, Aunt Olga and G. Leuchtenberg. In the afternoon Papa went to Petersburg. We walked with Aunt Olga and watched the Infantry regiment practice. Tatiana rode in a real carriage for the first time. It was over 10 degrees in the shade, very warm, feels like summer. Mama sat on the balcony. Aunt Olga and Papa had tea with her. Papa went to Grandmama's for dinner. Aunt Olga stayed until 9 and played kolorito with Mama.

Friday. 5 April. Had lessons. Had breakfast with Papa, Mama and Arseniev. In the afternoon [we] broke the ice. [It was] a bit windy, 7 in the shade, sunny. Had dinner with Mama and played kolorito with her in the evening. Papa went to [see] the 4th Infantry regiment. After that he will go hunting for wild grouse.

Saturday. 6 April. Had lessons. At 11 o'cl. we 5 went to the Manege[110] with Papa for the Svodny Cossack regiment parade. Very nice. Papa and Aleksei were wearing the Urals uniforms. Had breakfast with Mama and Nastenka. In the afternoon broke the ice with Papa. Sunny, warm, more than 15 degrees. Had tea with Papa and Mama. Had dinner with them and Count Grabbe. Everyone went to vsenoshnaya. So nice. Darling Mama also came and got tired.

---

[109] Dice, literally translated as "bones".
[110] An arena or enclosed area in which horses and riders are trained.

Sunday. 7 April. At 10 ½ went to obednya at the regimental church. After that there was a big breakfast. Dear AKSHV was there. [I] stared at his back from far away the entire time. Then [we] went out on the balcony. It was very bright, sunny, warm and windy. Went to see Derevenko[111], who finally returned from the hospital. Varvara Yuvchenko's son Evgeny, my godson, was there. So sweet. He is 4 months old. Mama rode in the park in an equipage. We walked around the garden breaking the ice. Irina and [her] brothers had tea with us. After that we saw a cinematograph. Had dinner with Papa, Mama, Irina, Fedor and Nikita[112]. After that Proskudin-Gorsky[113] showed us interesting color photos. Went to bed after 11. Mama was tired.

---

[111] Probably Derevenko, Aleksei's "Dyadka" – sailor nanny, who shared the same surname with the court physician V.N. Derevenko.

[112] Nikita was another one of Irina's brothers, and Olga's first cousin.

[113] Sergey Prokudin-Gorsky (1863-1934) A contemporary photographer famous as a pioneer of color photography

Olga and Aleksei with Pierre Gilliard (left) and sailor Derevenko

Monday. 8 April. In the morning rode with Madame Conrad[114]. In the morning and the evening we 5 went to the lower church. The doctor did not allow Mama to go. Had breakfast, tea and dinner with Papa and Mama. In the afternoon broke the remaining ice. It was sunny, and then suddenly it rained, although it was warm and clear.

---

[114] French tutor

Tuesday. 9 April. Rode with M.[adame] Conrad - nice weather. In the morning we 5 went to the lower church with Papa, also in the evening with Mama. Had breakfast and dinner with them, Aunt Ksenia and Uncle Sandro. In the afternoon climbed up the white tower with Papa. So beautiful. After that we visited Derevenko and broke the ice for a bit. Mama was tired. I played kolorito with her.

Wednesday. 10 April. Stayed in bed in the morning. Bekker came. Went to the lower church with Mama, Papa and Aunt Olga. Had breakfast and tea all together. 20 [degrees] in the sun. In the afternoon sat on the balcony and baked in the warmth. Poor Mama was very tired. Her heart is enlarged, and her kidneys ache, besides that she had a very busy day. In evening went to church with her. Had dinner with Papa and Mama. Confessed in their bedroom at 10 o'clock.

Thursday. 11 April. At 9 o'clock received communion in the small chapel. A few regiment officers were there too. After that [we] rode with Nastenka. Wonderful weather. Had breakfast, tea and dinner with Papa and Mama. In the afternoon I stayed on the balcony and baked in the sun. Mama also was lying out there for a bit. She does not feel well. Her back aches a lot. There was a Reading of the 12 Scriptures upstairs. Towards the end, with great joy I unexpectedly saw dear AKSHV. [We] returned with lit candles.

[Good] Friday. 12 April. In the morning rode with T and Trina. [It was] warm and nice. Had breakfast, tea and dinner with Papa and Mama. At 2 o'clock went to church for the Lifting of the Shroud[115]. Dear AKSHV was there too. In the afternoon sat with Mama on the balcony. Went to bed at 9 o'cl., because at 4 in the morning we will go to the regimental church for the Burial [of the Shroud][116].

Holy Saturday. 13 April. We 3 and Papa got up at 4 in the morning and went to the Svodny regiment church. When we walked around the church with the Shroud, dear AKSHV carried the Holy banner. It was very nice. It was warm. We took a nap after that. At 11 1/2 [we] went to obednya. In the afternoon we 4 and Mama went to Anya's to color eggs. N.P., Voronov, Rodionov, Kozhevnikov, Lili Dehn and Isa[117] were there. It was lots of fun. Papa arrived in time for tea. Had dinner with Papa and Mama. I received such delightful presents from everyone: a ring with fresh water pearls, earrings with aquamarine [stones], a royal hat, etc. Mama was very tired and did not feel well. At 11 ½ everyone went to zautrennya[118]. It was so beautiful and nice. There were a lot of flowers by the iconostasis, all the candles were lit. The church was full of Cossacks (all 300 were there, except for the ones on duty) and soldiers. The procession was beautiful with lanterns and fireworks. Everything was very, very nice, but I felt a little sad, because AKSHV was not there. After that [I] talked with Papa and Mama. At 3 ½ went to bed.

---

[115] The ceremony of the Service of Good Friday

[116] The ceremony of the Service of Holy Saturday

[117] Sophia Buxhoeveden, lady in waiting.

[118] In the Orthodox practice, the Service of Easter begins with "Zautrenniye" or the matins service, and the liturgy lasts overnight, ending with a full meal after the service. Olga retired at 3.30 in the morning on Easter Sunday.

"There were a lot of flowers…". Olga loved flowers - many years after her death dried flowers were found amidst the pages of her diaries.

Sunday (Christ's Resurrection). 14 April. At 11 there was Khristovanie[119] and

triple kisses. Poor Mama was awfully tired. I was happily anticipating [to see]

---

[119] Traditional Easter greetings

AKSHV on this day but he was not there, of course. So awfully tiresome. Had breakfast, tea and dinner with Papa and Mama. In the afternoon T and I kayaked. It was sunny and warm, but suddenly it rained a little. [...]. At 7 o'clock [we] went to vsenoshnaya, and my friend was not there again. Went to bed before 10.

Monday. 15 April. Went to obednya. Towards the end there was a procession with stops facing 4 different directions. Had breakfast and tea with Papa and Mama. At 2 o'cl. went to the Grand Palace for Easter greetings with the entire Imperial Court, all the commanders, soldiers and Cossacks[120]. After that kayaked until 5. It was sunny, but cooler. At a quarter to 8, we 2 and Papa went to Grandmama's in Petersburg. Had dinner and tea with Grandmama and darling Aunt Olga. After that Aunt Ksenia, Irina and her 2 brothers came over. [We] left after 10. Mama has a severe headache and does not feel well.

Tuesday. 16 April. At 11 all 5 of us and Papa went to watch the Grenadier Regiment parade. It was sunny and rather warm in the sun. Dear AKSHV was there. I was so happy to see him (he was wearing red and white) Had breakfast with Mama and Aunt Olga. Had tea with them and Papa. In the afternoon climbed up the white tower with Papa and Aunt Olga, watched the Infantry practice and kayaked. Mama's headache is better, thank God. She was lying down on the balcony. Had dinner with her and Papa, who read in his [room] until 10 o'cl. 45

---

[120] At this important court occasion, the Emperor and Empress kissed each member of the court three times, and handed out porcelain easter eggs. The ceremony was especially large during the Tercentenary. In 1913, Olga stood in for the Empress, who was ill.

min. In the afternoon bid Easter greetings to dear N.P. and Anya. It was so nice. It is his birthday today, he turned 33[121].

Wednesday. 17 April. At 11 o'clock we 5 and Papa went to watch the 1st and 2nd infantry Regiment parade. It is cold but clear today. We 5 had breakfast by ourselves. Mama stayed in her room. She had a severe headache. At 1 o'clock we 4 went to the [illeg] house to celebrate Christ's resurrection. At 2 o'cl. we went to Petersburg with Trina. Sat with Grandmama and Aunt Ksenia for a little bit. At 3 o'cl. went to Aunt Olga's with her. At 3 o'cl. 15 min. AKSHV ([who was] wearing light gray and black), Yuzik, Skvortsov and Zborovsky arrived. We sat cozily, did not talk much. At tea I sat between AKSHV and Skvortsov, as usual. At 4 o'cl. Rodionov, Klyucharev, N.P., Sasha with his mother, Irina and Fedor [all] arrived. Uncle Petya and Kulikovsky were there too. After that [we] played rope in the spare dining room. [It was] such fun. Then we played turkey, slap-on-hands, falcon, tag, etc. in the hall, taking breaks after each game. At dinner I sat between my two most favorite officers: N.P. and AKSHV. I was terribly happy. Then [we] talked in Aunt Olga's [room] until 8 o'cl. Mama's headache is better, thank God, but she was lying down in the dark. Anya and I sat with her until 10 o'cl. Papa had dinner with his 1st Infantry regiment. Al[ksei] has a sore throat. [His] temperature [is] 37.9. AKSHV's birthday – 25 July, name day – 30 August.

---

[121] She is probably referring to N.P. Sablin here.

Olga and Tatiana with their father and officers

Thursday. 18 April. Rode with Trina and after 11 went to the Nanny school[122] to greet [them] with Christ's Resurrection. Stayed there until 12 o'cl. 45 min., played with the adorable little children. Had breakfast with Papa and Kostya. Mama stayed on her sofa. Had dinner with the same. In the afternoon walked with Papa, kayaked and rode bicycles for the first time. The sun is shining, the sky is blue. Had tea with Papa and Mama. Her headache is better, thank God. At 8 o'clock Grigori Yefimovich came over, we all sat together, [it was] very nice. Papa

[122] Orphanage

read S.S. Pogulyaev's letter. In the morning saw Count Nirod and the Calvary regiment recruits from far away.

"... Rode bicycles for the first time". Olga on a bicycle with Anastasia on foot." Shadows of the other two girls can be seen walking in front of them.

Friday. 19 April. At 11 went to see the 1st Cavalry division and infantry regiment parade. Had breakfast with Papa, Mama and Gavril. At 2 o'cl. we 5 and Papa went to the Svodny regiment barracks for soldier games. It was lots of fun. The dear ones were having such fun. There were lots of games with prizes. At the end dear AKSHV arrived (wearing crimson and black). I had hoped [I would] see

103

him and felt very happy. After we returned, I sat with Ira[123]. At 5 o'cl. Nastasia and I went to Anya's. Countess Kleinmichel[124] with Tata[125] and Olga[126] were there. We had tea and stayed there until 7 o'cl. Papa had dinner with the 2nd Infantry regiment. We had dinner with Mama and Gavril. She has a headache and is not feeling well.

Saturday. 20 April. Rode with Trina and at 11 went to the nanny school. Played with the little children. Had breakfast and tea with Papa, Mama and Aunt Olga. It was cold and kept raining. In the afternoon we 5 went to the Svodny regiment barracks with Papa and Aunt Olga. They had games for the second half of the soldiers. Stayed there until 4 o'cl. 45 min. It was 3 degrees. Went to vsenoshnaya at the regimental church. Grigori Yefimovich stood at the altar. Had dinner with Papa and Mama. In the evening sat with Mama and worked. She does not feel well. Papa read in his [room].

Sunday. 21 April. Rode with Trina before obednya. It was awfully cold. After church we planted trees. Had a big breakfast. AKSHV was there. At 2 o'cl. 7 min Nastenka, Trina and I went to Petersburg. Anastasia has a sore throat, temperature 37.1, and stayed home. Mama's heart is enlarged, she has a headache and is lying down on the sofa. [We] went to Grandmama's. Aunt

---

[123] Most likely "Ira" was Irina Sheremetieva, wife of Count Dimitri Sheremetiev, the Tsar's childhood friend and aide-aide-camp

[124] Countess Marie Kleinmichel

[125] Probably nickname for "Natalia".

[126] Olga Kleinmichel, the Countess's daughter, later married Officer Pavel Voronov, Olga's love interest.

Ksenia and Vasia were there. [We] left at 3 o'cl. At 3 o'cl. 15 min., Skvortsov, AKSHV and Zborovsky came over to the Aunt's house. We sat together as usual. Had tea on the little balcony. I sat with AKSHV as usual. And also sat with him at dinner, as well as with Zborovsky. After that we played rope, slap-on-hands, tag, and again rope in the spare dining room. Countess of Leuchtenberg with Sasha and Kolya, Irina, Fedor, Klyucharev, Rodionov, Kulikovsky and Shangin were also there. It was lots of fun. After dinner and until 8 o'cl. we sat and stood in Aunt Olga's study. I was talking with dear AKSHV very cozily. Returned with Olga Yevgenievna Byutsova. Sat with Mama until 10 o'cl. Papa read. His right shoulder hurts. Aunt had the phonograph turned on: "Do Not Tempt Me", "Doubt" by Glinka, "In Church" by Tchaikovsky, etc., until 8 o'clock.

Monday. 22 April. The lessons started. Had tea with Papa and Mama, had dinner and breakfast with them and Ioannchik. In the afternoon rode bicycles with Papa – [it was] very cold. In the morning there was snow everywhere. Tried on hats from 4 until 5. So tiresome. We three went to vsenoshnaya at the regimental church. In the evening stayed with Mama. Papa read.

Tuesday. 23 April. At 11 [we] went to the Regimental church for obednya. After that there was moleben. Later Grandmama, Aunt Olga, Aunt Ksenia with [their] husbands and others had breakfast. All the officers of the Guard and Svodny regiment stood outside of the church. In the afternoon [we] rode bicycles everywhere with Papa. After that we kayaked around the pond [...]. Had tea and dinner with Papa and Mama. At 8 o'cl. N.P. came over to greet Mama. [I] saw him for only a minute.

Wednesday. 24 April. Had lessons. We 2 rode with Trina. Had breakfast with Papa, Mama and Daragan. In the morning Papa and I rode our bicycles around Tablovo and kayaked around the pond. It is warm today. Had tea with Papa and Mama. Nastaska's temperature [was] 38.2 in the evening, her tonsils are swollen. Papa had dinner in Peterhof with the Ulan regiment. We had dinner with Mama and Irina, who is leaving.

Olga on a bicycle

Thursday. 25 April. Had lessons. Had tea with Papa and Mama. Had breakfast and dinner with them and Sergei. Nastaska is in bed. Her temperature [was] 37.9 in the evening. In the morning and the afternoon Mama was lying down on the balcony. It is warmer. We three and Papa rode our bicycles past Tablovo along the Krasnoselskoe highway and stretched out on the grass by the railroad. Kayaked around the pond. Went to bed at 10 o'cl.15 min. Mama No.2 ½ .

Friday. 26 April. Had lessons. Had breakfast with Papa, Mama and Sashka V. Dinner with them and Anya. Nastasia is still in bed, but her temperature is normal. 25 degrees in the sun. In the morning and afternoon Mama was lying down on the balcony. Her heart is enlarged and she has a headache. Rode our bicycles around Tablovo with Papa. Warm and nice. The Count played cards with Sashka and Anya.

Saturday. 27 April. Had lessons. At 11 o'cl. Papa, Aleksei and I went to see the Imperial Artillery parade. It was very nice. Saw N.P. and his brother. Had breakfast with Mama, tea - with her and Papa, dinner - with them and Sandro. In the afternoon walked with Papa, and then kayaked around the pond and through the flood gate. Mama was not there in the morning and afternoon because she was not feeling well. Went to vsenoshnaya at the regimental church. The Cossacks sang.

Sunday. 28 April. At 10 ½ went to obednya. Dear AKSHV was there too. After

molebna there was a big breakfast. [They] played music. After that [we] stayed

on the balcony, very warm: 27 in the sun. It was silly: at first nobody stood next to

us, but then the Svodny regiment officers were called, and we talked a little. I

saw my friend from far away only, and not the entire time. He is so sweet, he

smiled a little. In the afternoon Mama [rode] in an equipage. We 4 picked flowers

with Papa and Anya for poor Aunt Olga. We went to see her today, because our

Mrs. Franklin[127] died at 4 in the morning. So sad. May God grant her strength.

After that [we] kayaked and rode our bicycles. Had tea on the balcony, dinner

inside with Papa and Mama. Worked in the evening. Went to bed at 10 o'clock.

Monday. 29 April. Had lessons. Had breakfast with Papa, Mama and Nikolai M.

7 degrees in the shade, chilly and windy, but rather clear. In the afternoon we 4

and Papa rode our bicycles on the [Chidren's?] Island and everywhere, then we

kayaked. Had dinner with Mama and Anya and spent the evening all together. I

spoke to N.P. on the telephone. Papa went to Grandmama's.

Tuesday. 30 April. Had lessons. Had breakfast with Papa, Mama, Aunt Ducky[128],

Uncle Kyrill, Uncle Boris and Dmitri. Mama and Aleksei stayed in the study. In the

afternoon we 4 walked around the park with Papa and Anya, Mama [rode] in the

carriage. It was cold, but sunny. Then [we] kayaked. It was just 1 degree. It

---

[127] Mrs Franklin was Olga Alexandrovna's former nanny.
[128] Nickname of Grand Duchess Victoria Melita, wife of Grand Duke Kyrill Vladimirovich.

snowed and hailed. Had dinner with Papa and Mama. Then Mama read "Notes by Empress Elizaveta". Then Papa went off to read, and we worked until 10 o'cl.

Family gathering. Left to right: Tatiana, Duchess Maria Antonia of Mecklenburg-Schwerin, "Aunt Ducky", Olga. Sitting: Grand Duchess Maria Pavlovna the Elder, Alexandra, Nicholas. Back row: Grand Duke Kirill Vladimirovich, Princesses Elizabeth and Olga of Greece

~

May

Wednesday. 1 May. Had lessons. Had breakfast and tea with Papa, Mama and Aunt Olga. Had dinner with them and Count Grabbe. It is cold today, it snowed in the morning. 6 [degrees] in the afternoon, 0 degrees in the evening. Walked to Tablovo with Papa and Aunt Olga. Then kayaked around the pond. Until 6 o'cl. frame embroidered with Aunt Olga at Mama's. Mama's heart [is] No.2. Papa received 30 people in the morning. I have a runny nose.

Thursday. 2 May. Had lessons. It is warmer today: 10 in the morning. Had breakfast with Mama. Papa went to the 4th Infantry regiment church consecration. Waited for Nastasia for a long time. Walked and stopped by to see Derevenko. Varvara Yuvchenko was there with Evgeny. He was sleeping – such a darling. Then we rode bicycles and double boats and watched pikes and perches with her and Derevenko, then it rained for a long time. Had tea with Papa and Mama. Had dinner with them and Uncle Petya.

Friday. 3 May. Had lessons. Had breakfast with Papa and Mama. Had dinner with them and Count of Leuchtenberg. In the afternoon Nastasia, Papa and I went to the consecration of Russia's Warriors. After that [we] rode our bicycles and then double boats with Derevenko and V. N. Derevenko[129]. 7 [degrees] in the evening. Nothing interesting happened today.

Saturday. 4 May. Had lessons. After the parade there was a big breakfast for the Ulans[130]. We 4, Papa and Mama were there, as well as the regiment ladies. I sat at the table with Nastasia, Prince Eristov, Apukhtin, PrinceTrubetskoy and his wife, Madame Skalon and some other officers. There was music. A, Papa and I took a walk, climbed up the white tower and kayaked. Warm, windy. Had tea with Papa and Mama. Had dinner with them and Arseniev. Mama was very tired, poor thing. [I] stayed home, but Papa went to vsenoshnaya.

"Had lessons". Tatiana and Olga at their lesson

---

[129] Aleksei's sailor nanny and one of court physicians shared a family name, but were not related.
[130] One of the regiments

Sunday. 5 May. Went to vsenoshnaya at the regimental church. After the service there was a big breakfast. Talked on the balcony. It was awfully hot in the sun. Dear sweet AKSHV was there. Bright blue eyes. In the afternoon walked with Papa and Aunt Olga. After that she and I rode around Gatchinka. N.P. was also there in a double boat with the sisters. In the morning [it was] 25 in the sun. Had tea with Papa, Mama and Aunt Olga. Poor darling Mama is not feeling well, her heart is enlarged. [Her] temperature was 37.2 in the morning. Oh Lord, save her. At 6 o'cl. went to Aunt Olga's and stayed there together. Had dinner with Papa, Aunt Olga, Grandmama, Aunt Ksenia, Uncle Petya and Uncle Sandro. Mama was in her [room]. At 9 ½ went to the Circular hall to see Andreyev's balalaika players. They played so well. I sat with dear N.P. the whole time. Went to bed at 11 o'cl. 15 min. (felt very happy). Had tea with Mama, Papa and [illeg.]

Monday. 6 May. In the morning went to Aunt Olga's, and Uncle Petya, the General, then went to Grandmama's. At 11 o'cl. we 4 went to the Grand Palace with Papa. Walked to church arm-in-arm with the relatives to obednya. I was [walking] with U[ncle] Nikolai[131]. There were a lot of people. Dear N.P. and AKSHV were there. After the service there was baisemain[132] and a big breakfast – very nice. Poor darling Mama is not feeling well. Heart is No.2 and because of that her temperature was 37.2 in the morning, 37.4 in the afternoon and 37.1 in the evening. She got up for tea and for dinner. In the afternoon [we] rode bicycles

[131] Probably H.I.H. Grand Duke Nikolai Nikolaevich of Russia
[132] Kissing of hands

and kayaked with Papa. A very warm wind. In general I was happy with today. Listened to music at the pavilion. Sat with Papa and Mama until 10 o'cl. They responded to telegrams.

Tuesday. 7 May. Had lessons. At 12 ½ we 5 and Papa went to the regimental church for the farewell moleben. [There were] so many candles, the Cossacks and soldiers, all officers of the guard and the Svodny regiment. Dear AKSHV was also there. [It was] overcast but warm. In the evening [it] rained a lot. Had breakfast, tea and dinner with Papa and Mama. In the afternoon we 4 and Papa stopped by the banner. Then we walked, kayaked. [I] went home because of Bekker and sat with Mama and Anya on the balcony. After dinner [I] sat with Papa and Mama. At 10 ½ we 2 went to see off dear Papa. He went to Berlin for the Emperor's daughter's wedding. Very sad. May the Lord save him. Count Nirod went with him. May the Lord save Mama too.

Olga and Tatiana.

Wednesday. 8 May. [There were] no lessons. The teachers did not come. I stayed in bed, read and worked. Had breakfast with Mama. Had tea and dinner with her and Anya. It rained in the morning but was warm and sunny in the afternoon. [We] tried on dresses. After that we 4 and Nastenka went to the Nanny school. Played with the children in the gazebo. Mama has a headache and is not feeling well. Thank God [we] received good news from Papa. Mama got two telegrams.

Thursday. 9 May. From 9 o'cl. 15 min. until 10 o'cl. [I] sat on the balcony with T and baked in the sun. After that had lessons. Had breakfast with Mama and Aunt Olga. In the afternoon we 4 and Aunt Olga went riding. We rode by the church, the barracks and the Assembly ([I] hoped to see my dear) and got lucky. AKSHV and a bunch of other officers were on the balcony. So nice. At about 3 ½ met N.P. (it's his name day today) at Znamenie[133] and went to Mama's. Sat on the balcony and had tea cozily. Had dinner with Mama and spent the evening with her and Anya. Papa sent a lovely lilac bouquet and a letter to Mama from [Germany?]. He sent a telegram from Berlin.

Friday. 10 May. Had lessons. Had breakfast and dinner with Mama. Her heart is almost No.2. T. and I rode with Nastenka. [Today] was not as nice as yesterday: 15 degrees in the shade. Very nice and warm. Had tea at Anya's with Countess Kleinmichel, her son, Tata and Olga. After dinner sat with Mama. Papa sent me a telegram, he is very busy. Everything is well, thank God.

Saturday. 11 May. Had lessons. At 11 o'cl. we 2 and Lili Ob[olenskaya] went to Grandmama's at Anichkov in Petersburg. She was giving out awards and medals to the Women's Institute graduates. After that we had breakfast with them. Aunt Olga and Aunt Ksenia were there. Irina was there too. She returned with us and we had tea with Mama in the large sitting room. It rained heavily and [was] warm. Went to vsenoshnaya. Tomorrow is Germogen's[134] day. Had dinner with Mama and Anya. Then spoke to N.P. on the telephone. Mama stayed in her [room]. Good news from Papa. He is leaving at 9 o'cl. today.

---

[133] The Church of the Virgin of the Sign at Tsarskoe Selo

[134] Patriarch Hermogen of Moscow, who was killed by the Poles during the Time of Troubles was glorified by the Russian Orthodox Church in 1913

Sunday. 12 May. Went to obednya at the regimental church. AKSHV was there. [I] was very happy to see him, did not expect to. Had breakfast and dinner with Mama and Anya. [...]

Author's note: Some of the diary pages here are missing. At about this time, Olga and her family set out on progress around ancient Russian cities related to the founding of the Romanov dynasty, for the tercentennial celebrations.

Map of the cities Olga and her family visited by train and steamer during the tercentennial celebrations.

Olga and Tatiana

Thursday. 16 May. At 1 o'cl., after breakfast [we] arrived in Vladimir. 12 degrees in the shade, sunny, windy. Masses of people at the station, as usual. The guards from the 9th Grenadier Siberian Regiment were there. From there [we] rode in motors to the Uspensky Cathedral. Aleksei returned to Mama's who stayed in the train. Her heart was No.3. A little after 3 o'cl. [we] arrived in Suzdal. Went to their main cathedral, then the Rizopolozhensky and Spaso-Yefimovsky monasteries. Visited Count Pozharsky's[135] grave. We looked at the wonderful antiques and the beautiful vestry[136]. From there [we] went to the Pokrovsky monastery, where we had tea with the Matushka[137]. Also looked at the vestry (Shkudenadsky, Sherbakov). At 7 o'cl. arrived in Bogomolovo. The train stopped nearby. Went to see the wonderful monastery and the place where Saint Prince Andrei Bogolubsky[138] was killed. Papa received delegations from the local societies. Returned to the train at 8 o'cl. 5 min. In Vladimir, Mama received women with bouquets [of flowers]. On the way to Suzdal all the peasants we passed in the villages greeted Papa with crosses and church banners. There were tables set up in front of each house with bread-and-salt[139] and icons. Mama's heart is 3, not 2. [All is] well, thank God.

---

[135] Prince Dmitri Pozharsky was an aristocrat who fought to protect Nizhni Novgorod against Polish occupation, later becoming a national hero

[136] Room or building attached to a church, used as an office or for changing into vestments.

[137] Mother Superior - literally translated as "The Little Mother".

[138] Grand Prince of Vladimir-Suzdal in the 12th century. Was later canonized by Orthodox Church.

[139] Bread and salt is served to guests as a Russian ceremonial welcome

118

The imperial steamer "Mezhen"

Minin[140] on the Volga River. Friday. 17 May. At 10 o'cl [we] arrived in Nizhny

Novgorod. The honor guard from the 37th Ekaterinburg regiment was there. From

there we went to the Spaso-Preobrazhensky Cathedral. Troops were lined up

along the streets. Schools and gymnasiums were there too. After molebna Mama

and Aleksei went to the palace. We went down to Minin's grave, where a Litia[141]

was held. Then we walked in a procession to the site of the future monument for

Prince Pozharsky and Prince Minin. There was ceremonial marching. Went back

---

[140] Kuzma Minin, along with Dmitri Pazharsky, fought against Polish occupiers of Nizhni Novgorod.

[141] A prayer service.

to the palace and had breakfast. Mama and we 4 received the Matushka[142] and the ladies. Papa received the local leaders, then he went to visit the new bank. We stayed with Mama – she was very tired of course. May God grant her strength. At 4 ½ went to have tea with [the local] nobility. There were masses of people. I sat with Khvoshinsky's sister – she is very sweet. Then [we] went to the pier – [it was] far. The owners of The Volga shipbuilding factories with their families greeted us there, toasted to everyone's health, shouted "hurra", etc. Our steamer is awfully cozy. My cabin is portside, near Mama's cabin (Gulyga, Zborovoy, the good constable Shapkin). Cool, overcast. A big dinner was served in the "Tsar Mikhail Feodorovich"[143] dining hall. We 2 and Papa went to dinner. Appealing, big dining hall. A bit after 10 o'cl. we sailed off. Mama's heart No.3 – May God bless [her].

"Then we walked in a procession…" Olga and her family in Nizny Novgorod

---

[142] Mother Superior, literally "Little Mother"
[143] Mikhail Feodorovich was elected the first Romanov Tsar in 1613.

Same – along the Kama River. Saturday. 18 May. We proceeded along until 9 o'cl. 45 min. Now we stopped at the pier. It is very cold and windy. [We] walked on the deck, sat, went on deck-bridge, etc., had breakfast with Papa and everyone in the afternoon. Mama went upstairs to lie down in the cabin. The wind subsided by evening, it was sunny all day. Mama has a headache, her heart aches. Beautiful surroundings – masses of people. Went to bed at 11 o'cl. We were learning to curtsy in Mama's cabin. It was very funny.

"We walked on the deck." Olga (third from left), her sisters and some officers on "The Mezhen". Aleksei is on far right.

Sunday. 19 May. About 10 in the morning, after passing through Kostroma, [we] stopped at the pier, about 12 miles from the Ipatiev monastery. Warm, sunny and less windy. The honorary guard of the Yerivan regiment, and further down everyone was lined up along the streets. I was so happy to see old friends, especially Otar Purtzeladze, he is so sweet. The 183rd Pultusky regiment was there, the combat engineers, a hundred Kizlyars from the Grebensky regiment, [of] Tersky Army. They played [music] during breakfast. We were met by a procession and carried the icon to the cathedral with this procession, where obednya and moleben were held. Grigori Yefimovich was there, and all the relatives too. [We] went to a museum in Mikhail Feodorovich's palace and returned at about 4 o'cl. Went to Kostroma. Darling Mama got very tired of course. Went to the museum, after that – to a tea party at the Assembly of the Nobility. Then [we] returned to the Ipatiev pier. At 8 o'cl. there was a big dinner in the "Tsar Mikhail Feodorovich" dining hall. In the evening we 2 and Papa went to to the river bank to see the fireworks [along with] Skvortsov, Makikha, Pankratov and Shkuropadsky.

"Went to Kostroma." Olga and her family at the Ipatiev Monastery in Kostroma.

Monday. 20 May. At 10 o'cl. [we] went to the cathedral. On the way there Papa got out and greeted the troops. From the cathedral the procession went to the site of the future monument. Molebna was held and stones were laid. Sunny, a bit windy, nice. The Yerivansky, Pultusky and Grebensky regiments performed ceremonial marching. From there Papa went to the Provincial garden to receive the local leaders, etc. We 5 with Mama and Aunt Ella went to the Bogoyavlensky Monastery. There was an obednitza at the church. We received wonderful gifts from the nuns and crafts made by school children. Matuska Suzanna served us tea, paskha[144] , etc. Then Mama received the ladies. Last to come in with flowers were M. Ledivali with some rather nice members of the Yerivansky regiment. I got flowers from Otar Purtzeladze. G. Ravdopulo, Count V. Sido [illegible], Eristov and two more were there too. I was so happy to see them, they are so sweet. Had breakfast at about 3 o'cl.. At 3 ½ we went to see an interesting old church "Spas na Debryakh[145]." Then we visited the new Red Cross and the local exhibition and then had tea with everyone. Very tiring, masses and masses of people came to see us off. Returned to the Ipatiev pier. At 8 o'cl. a big dinner was served in the Tsar Mikhail Feodorovich dining hall. Heavy rain, warm wind. Sat with Mama until 11 o'cl. She was very tired, heart No.2. [We] left at 10 o'cl. The local officers escorted us upstairs in spite of the rain. Gr[igori] Yef[imovich] and Father Vornavoy were in the cathedral. It is such a shame that this is our last night on "The Mezhen".

---

[144] A traditional Russian Easter dessert made from sweetened cheese, and eggs.
[145] "The Savior on the Rubble"

Aerial photo of the imperial family's visit to Kostroma on 20 May, 1913.

Tuesday. 21 May. On the train to Yaroslavl, 12 o'cl. 20 min. in the morning.

Arrived here at 9 o'cl. [It is] very warm but windy. An honor guard of the 181st

Ostrolensky regiment met us at the pier. Rashpil and AKSHV were there. Yuzik

was [on guard] by the Uspensky Cathedral. From there we went to the Church of

Ioann the Baptist, a very interesting old church. Before that we went to the [illeg]

Church (AKSHV), where the Icon of the Savior is kept (the one that saved the

city from the plague). Then we visited the Spassky Monastery, where we saw the

vestry and the living quarters of Mikhail Feodorovich, where he stayed for 26

days after the coronation. From there we went to the Ilyinsky church, and again

125

looked at the antiques. (AKSHV). Returned after 1 o'clock, had breakfast with masses of people in the Tsar Mikhail Feodorovich dining hall. Mama and Al[eksei] returned from the cathedral. After 3 o'cl. we 4 and Papa went to the consecration ceremony of an orphanage commemorating the 300th anniversary. From there we went to the Exhibit of Yaroslavl Province's manufacturing. Masses of gifts, [we] got very tired, [it was] very long and boring, also very hot. At 5 o'cl. 15 min. [we] went to the Tolgsky Monastery. Very beautiful (AKSHV). Mama and Al.[eksei] came too. Moleben, vestry. Returned and had dinner in the middle of the river, a little farther. Heavy rain, thunderstorm, gusts. Returned at 9 o'cl. At 10 o'cl. we went to the Assembly of the Nobility with Papa and Mama. Zbruyeva, Sobinov, the quartet, N.P. performed very well. It was hot, had tea. The gymnasium students sang. At 12 o'cl. we were [back] on the train. The good sweet AKSHV was there. I was terribly happy to see him. Poor Mama got very tired. Heart No.3, aches. May the Lord save her.

In Yaroslavl

Wednesday. 22 May. 9 o'cl. Rostov, 10.45. Left at 9 o'clock, arrived in Rostov at 10 o'cl. Very warm, more than 20 [degrees] in the sun, but windy and dusty. Mama did not go anywhere and spent the entire day in bed. She has tonsillitis, [her] temperature 37.8, 38.4, 38.7, 38.8, sore throat and headache. Heart is 1. So sad. May the Lord save her. We went to the Uspensky Cathedral, listened to the bell chimes, walked around the kremlin[146] and looked at the vestry in one of the churches on the way. Returned for breakfast (Shkuropadsky, Sherbatov). At 2 o'cl. unexpectedly saw AKSHV (in a red uniform) and Yuzik from far away through a window. I felt awfully happy. They left a few minutes later. We five and

---

[146] Every ancient Russian city had its own "kremlin"

Papa went in motors to the Yakovlevsky M[onastery], which is very beautiful. Also visited the old Church of Ioann the Baptist on the Ishma River. It was built in 1687. In the morning we also stopped at the Blagoveshensky Church, which has the miraculous Icon of Adoration and saw the girl who was healed. Had tea at home. Went to vsenoshnaya at the Church of the Resurrection. After dinner sat with Mama.

"Arrived in Rostov..."

Thursday. 23 May. The Ascension. At 10 o'cl. arrived in Petrovsk. On the way to church Papa received the local leaders. Went to obednya at the Town Church. Returned for breakfast. Mama's temperature was 37.6, 37.4, 37.5 in the morning. Her heart aches, she has a headache and sore throat, but not too bad. Around 2 o'cl. Anastasia, Papa, the sisters, Nastenka and I went to Pereslavl in motors.

Visited Nikitsky, Danilovsky and Feodorovsky monasteries. The old nun, 86 years old, blessed us. Then [we] visited estates of the Vladimir nobility. Warm, overcast, a little windy. Rain, [wind] gusts in the distance. Masses of people. Papa went down to the Pereslavl lake and watched the funny performers. Had tea inside. On the way back stopped at the Church of Life-Giving Trinity. Smoked. Left very soon. Anya was also there. She came to see Mama for an hour. Aleksei's arm hurts, he is crying the poor boy (Gulyga, Zborovsky). Pereslavl - (Shkuropadsky, Beliy). Petrovsk.

Olga and Tatiana with their parents during the tercentennial celebrations

Friday. 24 May. Moscow. At 10 o'cl. [we] arrived at the Troitze-Sergiyevsky Monastery. Went to obednya, reveled the relics, had tea with the Metropolitan.

Wonderful weather (Zborovsky, Beliy and Sherbakov). At 3 ½ arrived in Moscow. Stopped by different houses. We 4 with Aunt Ella, Papa, the relatives, the Imperial suite [were] on horseback. A hundred Guards at the front. Dear AKSHV smiled across the crowd. N.P., the good B.-B., Count Nirod were [all] there. Very nice in general.The Sumsky regimental squadron followed [us] in the back. Obednya or Litia, not sure, was held at the Arkhangelsk Cathedral. Papa lit the oil burner under the tomb of the tsars, then walked back. Had tea with Papa, Mama, Aunt Olga and Aunt Ksenia. Poor Mama was very tired. Temperature 37.2 in the morning, heart 2.5. Had dinner with Papa and Aunt Ksenia. Mama was in bed. May the Lord save her. Gr[igori] Ye[fimovich] was standing outside the cathedral.

"We 4 with Aunt Ella..." during tercentennial celebrations.

Saturday. 25 May. [We] came in to greet and give good wishes to Mama in the morning. Poor darling, she does not feel well at all. Her temperature is not back to normal yet, heart No.2 and [she is] very tired. At 11 o'cl. [we] made an appearance on the Red Balcony and then went to the Uspensky Cathedral. Masses of people, warm. Saw AKSHV and darling N.P., same as yesterday. Went to the Chudov Monastery to see the Holy Martyr Aleksei. There was a family breakfast. Mama went to lie down. At 3 o'cl. we four and Papa went to the Chudov Monastery to look at the beautiful antiques. Had tea – the Matushka of the Voznesensky Monastery served [it to] us. From there we went to see Saint Germogen's tomb. Then [we] went to see the house of Romanovs. Had tea with Papa, Maria and Dmitri. Her little son Leonard[147] was there too. A massive dinner was served, toasted to everyone's health, then there were fireworks, etc. I walked and sat with Uncle Petya. Then [I] sat with Mama, Aunt Olga and Aunt Ella, [and] had tea. At dinner we wore Russian [traditional] dresses.

---

[147] H.R.H. Prince Gustaf Lennart of Sweden, Duke of Småland, son of H.I.H. Grand Duchess Maria Pavlovna (the younger) and her then husband, H.R.H. Prince Willem of Sweden, Duke of Sodermanland. Maria and Wilhelm would divorce in 1914.

"At dinner we wore Russian dresses." Olga in a traditional Russian dress.

Sunday. 26 May. At 11 o'cl. we 4 and Papa went to the Novospassky Monastery for obednya. Aleksei came towards the end, for Litia[148]. [We] went to see the ancestor tombs downstairs. Gr[igori] Yef[imovich] was there. Had breakfast at Aunt Ella's with Papa and Aunt Olga. Came back and in a ¼ hour went to the municipal council. Had tea there and accepted gifts. From a window watched the

---

[148] "Litiya" is a service held after liturgy or vespers to commemorate departed family members.

boys perform gymnastics. Had tea with Papa, Mama and Aunt Ella. After that S.I. came over with her sister and nephew. Had dinner with Papa and Mama and at 10 o'cl. went to the Assembly of the Nobility ball. AKSHV was there. The polonaise started, I walked in with Troyanov. It was very beautiful. I danced a lot. Once with N.P. and once with dear Otar Purtzeladze. Was very happy to see the Yerivansky regiment officers, unexpectedly. B.-B. and Count Nirod were there. Saw all my friends. During a quadrille saw AKSHV's sweet smiling face from far away. Very, very nice. Towards the end I just wanted to leave, had a peculiar feeling for some reason. Mama left earlier. We came back at 12 1/2. Wonderful warm weather. Thank you God for everything. Mama is tired.

Olga with her sisters and father inside the Moscow Kremlin

133

Monday. 27 May. On the train. We all got up late. At 11 we 4 went to the Armory Chamber to see the work by Stroganov school students, which will be sent to exhibit in Kiev in 3 days, I think. Then had breakfast with Mama, Aunt Ella and Maria. Papa had a big breakfast. Then returned to the exhibit with Marie, and then we 2 went to Marie's to see Mary and Olga Kleinmichel (stopped in Bologoe). Around 4 o'cl. we went to the Voznesensky Monastery, and from there – to the railroad station. Very nice. I think I saw AKSHV in a red cap on one of the far away balconies. May God bless him. The dear Yerivansky Regiment was lined up along the way. Darling Ot[ar] P[urtzeladze] and the family were at the station, along with B.-B., Count Nirod, etc. After dinner [I] sat with Mama, smoked. She is very tired, and the train keeps jolting her. May God save her.

Tuesday. 28 May. Tsarskoe Selo. Arrived around 6 o'cl. At 10 1/2 went to church for moleben. Had tea with Papa and Mama. Had dinner and breakfast with them and Veselkin. In the afternoon first went through the gifts in the hall, then went out to the garden with Papa. Nastasia and I sailed in a double boat with Vl.[adimir] N.[ikolaevich] Derevenko. The garden is so beautiful now. Lilacs are in bloom. It rained occasionally and is rather cool. It was only 8 [degrees] in the evening. I was happy that Mama was back home, heart No.2. As for me, I would have done it all over again. Did not see anyone.

Wednesday. 29 May. Did not do anything in the morning. At 12 ½ molebna was held in honor of Tatiana[149]. Papa, Mama, we 5, Aunt Olga, Aunt Ksenia, Uncle Sandro with the family were all there. After breakfast all of them, except Irina and the young ones, left. Sailed in double boats, Papa kayaked. Then smoked and picked lilies-of-the-valley on the little island. Had tea with Papa, Mama and Irina. Had dinner without her. Cool, damp, partly sunny, and raining occasionally.

"Sat with Mama"

---

[149] Tatiana's birthday.

Thursday. 30 May. Had lessons: religion and German. Maria has a sore throat and was moved into a separate room. Temperature 38.7, 38.8, 38.4, 38.1. Had breakfast and tea with Papa and Mama. Had dinner with them and Aunt Mavra[150]. Mama slept well but was tired of course. In the afternoon sat on the balcony with Mama, then – with Nastasia and Derevenko. Pretty warm, wonderful lilac. Had a music lesson. Aleksei's temperature 38.2, also a sore throat.

Friday. 31 May. Had Russian and German lessons. The old Cossacks [who are] leaving the service were [standing] in front of the house. Papa handed out pins to them. I handed out cards. There were young soldiers from the Caucasus, a hundred [soldiers] from the Kubansky Regiment and a hundred from the Tersky regiment, as well as 2 new officers. Had tea with Papa and Mama. Had breakfast and dinner with them and Gavril. Marie's temperature: 36.9, 37.1, 36.3, 37.2; Aleksei's: 36.9, 36.8, 37.1 – [he is] better. In the afternoon Nastasia and I walked with Papa, sailed in double boats with Fedor. Raining and chilly.

---

[150] Grand Duchess Elizaveta Mavrikievna, wife of Grand Duke Konstantin Konstantinovich (KR).

"Had lessons": Olga at her studies. Of all her siblings Olga was considered to be the brightest student.

~

June

Saturday. 1 June. Had religion and German lessons. Cold and raining. At 10 o'cl.

had breakfast with Mama, Count Fredericks and Silaev. It was nice to hear about

the regiment. In the afternoon tried on my uniform, and then rode in an equipage

with Ulan[151]. I steered [it] myself. Papa had breakfast with the Hussars. Had tea

with him and Mama. Had dinner with them and Silaev. Smoked afterwards.

Before vsenoshnaya saw Gr[igori] Yef[imovich]. It was so nice in church,

everything was green. Maria is feeling better, she is up. Aleksei is too. Mama is

tired.

---

[151] "Ulan" One of Tatiana's nicknames, she was the honorary commander-in-chief of the Ulan regiment.

Olga and Maria

Sunday. 2 June. At 11 [we] went to the Izmailovsky regiment's and combat engineer battalion's parades. After that had breakfast with Mama and Aunt Mavra. Around 2 o'cl. we 4 and Anya went to Peterhof to Aunt Olga's. AKSHV, Yuzik, Skvortsov, Zborovsky, Rodionov, Klyucharev, Semyonov, T., Sh.[urik] and

Nik. Al. were already there. Sonia Dehn[152] was also there, but she left soon. We went to the beach and then to the park, walked through the entire park and returned. Aunt Ksenia stayed home with [her] 2 sons and Irina. Ran around in the garden and played tag, gorelki, rope, slap-on-hands, turkey and some other games, and also just sat. It was so nice. After tea and at dinner sat with the dear sweet AKSHV, was awfully happy ([he wore] a nice red uniform). Left at 9 o'cl. Anya followed us in a motor. Mama was very tired. Papa went to the Izmailovsky regiment for dinner. [It is] very warm.

Olga and Tatiana with "Aunt Olga"

[152] Lili Dehn's sister-in-law

Monday. 3 June. Such foul weather. We 4 went to obednya at the regimental church. Papa went to the Railroad Battalion parade. Had breakfast with Papa and Mama. Had tea and dinner with them and with Count Ignatiev[153]. In the afternoon they photographed us. I feel bored today. Mama was very tired.

Tuesday. 3 June. Peterhof. Got up late due to Bekker. Had breakfast with Papa, Mama and Bagration. At 2 o'cl. 10 min. went to Znamenie, and then to the [train] station. At 3 ½ arrived in Peterhof. Chilly, rather windy. Had tea with Papa and Mama, had dinner with them and Aunt Olga. Went to bed late. Papa read to us. Mama is well thank God. I am lodging in 2 rooms upstairs.

Wednesday. 5 June. Stayed in bed for a long time – the bed is so comfortable. At 12 ½ we 4 and Mama went to church for moleben in honor of Anastasia[154]. Had breakfast with Papa, Mama, Ioann and Uncle Nik.[olai Nikolaevich?]. In the afternoon rode with Anya. Chilly and raining. Had tea with Papa, Mama, Aunt Olga, Sonia Dehn and her little boy. Had dinner with Papa, Mama and Ioann. Mama was tired, she was so busy lately, hardly had any rest.

---

[153] Count Paul Nikolaevich Ignatiev (1870-1945), was appointed Assistant Miniaster of Agriculture in 1912, and Imperial Minister of Education in 1915.

[154] Anastasia's birthday.

Olga and Tatiana in Peterhof

Thursday. 6 June. Stayed in bed for a long time. Dr. Kolist[155] came over, picked at [my] teeth. Had breakfast with Papa, Mama, Aunt Ksenia, Uncle Sandro and the family. In the afternoon we 4 went to Aunt Olga's with Irina and the older boys in motors. Around 3 o'cl. AKSHV ([in] a red uniform), Yuzik, Skvortstov and Zborovsky arrived there. [We] ran around the garden, played gorelki, slap-on-

---

[155] One of imperial dentists

142

hands, rope and tag. [It was] such fun! Then had tea, I sat with AKSHV. [He is] such a darling. Then [we] went upstairs and played hide-and-seek in all the rooms there. Horsed around dreadfully, turned things upside down, especially this one big wardrobe. 10 people climbed inside it, and also on top, broke the doors, laughed and had lots of fun. Left at 7 o'cl. Dear AKSHV is leaving for the Caucasus on Saturday. May God keep him. Had dinner with Papa, Mama and everyone else. Papa read funny stories by Teffi[156] to us. Mama was very tired. She went to see Countess Hendrikova at Strelna[157] and of course was exhausted.

---

[156] "Teffi" Nadezhda Alexandrovna Buchinskaya (née Lokhvitskaya 1872-1952) was a satirical writer favored by the Tsar, and beloved by Russians for her work in the magazine "Satyricon".

[157] The name of a town and a Palace near Saint Petersburg occupied by the Konstantinovichi branch of the Romanoov family.

Olga in bed

Friday. 7 June. At 11 o'cl. we 4 went in motors to see Tatiana[158] in Strelna. Played with her son Teymuraz[159] for a long time. From there we went to see the Countess Hendrikova. Raining and 4 degrees, windy, foul. Had breakfast with Papa, Mama, Aunt Olga, Uncle Nik. and Dmitri. In the afternoon [we] stayed home, read, played the piano. Mama and Papa went to visit Aunt Mops. After

---

[158] Tatiana Konstantinovna, daughter of "Aunt Mavra" and "Uncle Kostya" (Grand Duke Konstantin Konstantinovich).

[159] Prince Teymuraz Bagration-Moukhransky was the son of H.H. Princess Tatiana Konstantinovna and her husband Prince Konstantin Bagration-Moukhransky.

144

they returned we had tea together. Had dinner with Mama. Papa went to [see] the Cavalry Grenadier regiment. Aunt Ksenia's 3 boys played with Aleksei.

Saturday. 8 June. Went horseback riding with Trina and Tatiana. Finally it got sunny and warm. Had breakfast with Papa, Mama and the Duke of Monaco. In the afternoon walked on the rocks. Papa sailed in a double boat. Mama went to Countess Hendrikova's. Around 4 o'cl. we 4 and Anya went to her [house]. Had tea and sat outside in the garden. After 4 ½ Otar Purtzeladze, Ravtopulo and Count Sidolin-Eristov [came over]. [It was] awfully nice. Anya took photographs of us. After we returned, [we] had tea and dinner with Papa and Mama. Went to vsenoshnaya. Mama has a sore throat, but her temperature is normal.

"Had tea and sat outside in the garden." Left to right: Anastasia (standing), Olga, Tatiana, Anna Vyrubova, Nicholas and Alexandra and some officers.

Standart[160] – Kronshtadt. Sunday. 9 June. At 11 o'cl. we 4 and Papa went to the Cavalry Grenadier regiment parade on the military field. After that there was a big breakfast, but we went back and had breakfast with Mama, Olga Yevg[enievna] and Count Apraksin. In the afternoon we 4 picked lilies-of-the-valley and baked in the sun. At 3 o'clock Aunt Olga came over. At 4 o'cl. we all went with her to "The Alexandria"[161]. B.-B. and others saw us off. […] In Kronshtadt we transferred to the yacht. I am so happy to be back on my beloved Standart. It is rather chilly, but clear. Had dinner all together, and then sat with Aunt Olga, N.P. and Rodionov in the navigator's cabin. At 11 o'cl. had tea in the dining room. At 8 o'cl. a moleben was held on the deck. Darling Mama was lying down, she has a severe headache. May the Lord save her. My cabin is so cozy.

---

[160] The main imperial yacht

[161] Another of the Imperial yachts.

Olga and her sisters on the Standart

Voyage on the Standart. Monday. 10 June. I didn't go to the flag ceremony, but heard the music though the half-port. At 10 o'cl. we 4 and Papa went to the Peterhof pier in a motorboat. From the pier we went to the cathedral[162] on horseback. The troops and sailors were lined up along the way. Sunny but chilly, [it] got warmer by evening, nice sunset. After the consecration of the cathedral [we] returned to the yacht and had breakfast. At about 2 o'cl. we went out to sea.

---

[162] The Naval Cathedral at Kronstadt. Constructed from 1903-1913, the extraordinary Byzantine revival style cathedral was considered one of Russias most beautiful modern churches.

The flag was raised, the fleet saluted. Excellent transfer. Did not do anything special, walked around the deck, sat in the cabin with Pavl. Al.[163] Rodionov and Sablin came. After tea played with Pavl. Al. and [other] friends, also watched Aleksei play with the boys. A little after six, [we] arrived at the old nice place and docked at the side. Molebna was held at 8 o'cl. Balalaikas were playing during dinner. After that [I] held watch with Pavl. Al. on deck. Mama was lying down in the cabin. N.P. was there, as well as Aunt Olga. Mama is better, thank God. In the afternoon she was lying down on the quarter-deck.

Olga with her sisters and father at the consecration of St. Nicholas Cathedral in Kronstadt on 10 June, 1913

---

[163] Pavel Alekseyevich Voronov, one of the Standart officers who later became one of Olga's romantic interests.

11 June. Tuesday. At 9 ½ we 4 with Trina, Nastenka and Pavl. Al. drove to
Tukholma Island in motors. It is shallow, and there are a lot of boulders. We were
able to get to the beach by walking on them. Sat on top of a rock. Aunt Olga, the
Count, Kuzminsky and Kartavtzov were there. Returned at 11 o'cl. [I] read and
got dressed until 12 1/2. Then had breakfast. The commanders of all vessels
were invited. Then everyone went ashore, but I stayed behind with Mama, to my
great joy. Sat with her on the quarter deck. Dear N.P. was also there, he helped
paste in album. Zelenetzky also stopped by. Had tea after 5 o'cl. when everyone
returned. The weather was wonderful, sunny, 14 degrees in the evening. After
the flag ceremony and dinner [we] went on deck with Pavl. Al. Mama was lying
down in the cabin, she was tired, heart No.2. She does not look good. May the
Lord save her.

"Sat on top of a rock."

Wednesday. 12 June. At 9 ½ we 4 with Nastenka, Trina and Kozhevnikov went ashore in a motorboat. There we met Aunt Olga, Knyazhich, Semyonov, and Tulupov on the rocks. We sat there, it rained, Semyonov read stories by Teffi to us. Returned by 11 o'cl. The officers of all the ships were invited to breakfast as usual. In the afternoon [we] went ashore with Papa, Aunt Olga, etc., near the telegraph. From there [we] walked to the village. There we stretched out on the grass in the sun by the church. So nice and warm. Returned to where Aleksei was playing with the boys. Maria and Mama were getting dressed. After tea [I] read. 14 degrees in the evening. N.P., Mama, Anya, T., U., Olga, Pavl. Al., Kozhevnikov, Knyazich, Nastenka were making [pillows?] out of beans on the deck. Lots of fun. Poor Mama was tired, I think [her] heart was enlarged.

Thursday. 13 June. We 4 with Nastenka, Trina and Babitzky went to the little island across from Tukholma, where we picked old lilies-of-the-valley. Aunt Olga was there with Knyazich, Khvoshinsky and Kartavtzov. We stretched out on the grass in the sun. Zein, the Governor-General of Finland, had breakfast. In the afternoon [we] rode with Papa in Padio. A lot of officers accompanied us. Walked along the beach to the old cove. Relaxed on the beach on boulders – fun! A is minding Mama. Darling Mama is not feeling well. Heart No.2, very tired and in pain. May the Lord help her. In the evening she did not stay up but went to bed. We 2 played forfeits with N.P., Pavl. Al., Anya, Kolesnikov. Arseniev and Kublitzky were also there. Laughed and cheated a lot during the game. Very warm: 14 degrees in the evening. Assessed the day. [I] wonder what dear AKSHV is doing?

Olga reading on a beach

Friday. 14 June. Did not go ashore. Papa kayaked, also after tea. At 12 o'cl. moleben was held for Maria's birthday. In the afternoon [we] rode in motors to play tennis. I played 4 sets with Zelenetzky against Anya and Kira N.[164], also played one set with him against Kira and Arseniev, [we] won all 5 sets. It was warm in the sun. M, A and Aunt Olga waded barefoot in the water and in the marsh. Papa played 6 sets against Pavl. Al. and Khvoshinsky with Rodionov. [I]

[164] Kiryll Naryshkin

151

read until dinner. Mama went out on the deck after breakfast and left at 6 o'cl. Heart No.3, [she] does not feel well and is tired. Spent the evening in bed. After dinner Papa played kosti with Zelenetsky, Nevyarovsky and Serg.[ei] Vas.[ilievich] Zl. We 4 talked with Pavl. Al. and Rodionov on the watch deck. It was drizzling and cloudy. Saw N.P. for a bit.

Saturday. 15 June. Did not go ashore in the morning. It was initially overcast but later became wonderfully sunny and warm. Papa kayaked. In the afternoon everyone went ashore, but I stayed on the yacht to my great joy. At first Mama was lying down on the deck, but then went downstairs and returned at about 4 o'cl. She was lying down on the quarter deck starboard. N.P. helped her paste [photographs] in the album. At first I read, but after 4 o'cl. Pavl. Al. began his watch, so how could I sit still – of course I had to talk to him. Vsenoshnaya on the afterdeck[165] was so nice. After dinner we 2 sat in the aisle between the chimney and telegraph with Pavl. Al. and Nastenka and chatted. Aunt Olga went to bed early. Mama did not get up for dinner – her heart aches, and her left arm too because of that. Papa played kosti. Exquisite beautiful sunset.

---

[165] An open deck toward the stern of a ship.

Olga and her sisters on the Standart

Sunday. 16 June. How wonderful the obednya was on afterdeck. Today at 10 ½ some crew members from all the ships came over. Then there was a big breakfast with all the commanders. In the afternoon [we] went ashore. Sunny and warm. Dark clouds in the distance. [...] Played 4 sets [of tennis]: 2 with B. Nalde (from "The Polar Star"[166]) against Anya and T. Sh.[urik?], Semyonov, of course lost. Played the other 2 sets with Zebrin, Nalde and A and vice versa, but still lost. Walked on the giant-steps[167] and [illeg.] – it was fun. Papa [played] with Rodionov, Zebrin, Khvoshinsky and Count Pototzky (Strashny). Strong eastern

---

[166] Dowager Empress Maria's yacht

[167] A swing-like game

wind. After tea [we] rowed in a double boat with Rodionov and T. Papa, Kira and

Pavl. Al. were in kayaks. Nice evening – Mama feels a little better, thank God. In

the afternoon she was lying down on the deck, but did not come up in the

evening. Aunt Olga went to a picnic, which is why she did not have dinner with

us. In the evening T and I played kosti on the quarter deck with Pavl. Al. and

Rodionov. Nastenka was sitting nearby – [it was] cozy. Saw N.P. for a bit. My eye

hurts.

Monday. 17 June. Sailed in a double boat with T and Papa through a beautiful

narrow channel with many boulders. Kira used a kayak. It is very warm in the

sun, even hot. Sat with N.P. at breakfast for the second time. Mama was lying

down on the deck and had dinner, but went to bed right after that: 37.3, 37.2, due

to heart [her] left arm hurts. In the afternoon [we] played 3 sets with Anya against

T. and Pavl. Al. [It was] strange but we won the last one. Papa [played] with

Rodionov, Khvoshinsky and Count Podruky. Then [we] walked on the giant

steps. Relaxed in the sun. Read after tea. Did not do anything after tea. It was

chilly out at sea in the afternoon, but got muggy by night time. Clouds and

thunderstorm in the distance.

"In the afternoon [we] played 3 sets with Anya..." Olga and Anna Vyrubova on a tennis court.

Tuesday. 18 June. Did not do anything in the morning. There were boating exercises. Papa kayaked. Warm wind, small waves. By breakfast time a tent was set up on the quarter deck, it was so cozy. In the afternoon [we] went ashore. Played 2 sets with Kozhevnikov against Zelenetzky and Neverovsky. After that he and Sablin taught me to walk on stilts, but nothing came of it. Returned earlier than usual and had tea in the saloon on the "Polar Star". Then played with the officers on afterdeck. [It was] awfully hot. Mama did not come out for dinner. Her heart is still enlarged, No.2 and a bit [more], and aching, which is why she spent the evening in bed. At 8 o'clock, a gale and heavy rain came out of nowhere, but then it cleared up. The balalaika players performed in the dining room. There was a gale again at a little past 10 o'cl. but then the wind subsided completely. It is 19 degrees in my cabin, it's 11 o'cl. 12 min. now. Stood on the deck with Pavl. Al., Rodionov, Aunt Olga and T, chatted, laughed. Then Aunt went downstairs to Mama's, and we went in the control room because of the rain. Played with Pavl. Al., Akulina, fools[168] and read fortunes for a bit. My dear N.P. is sad. May the Lord keep him. Moleben was on deck, but we did not go because of rain – such a shame. The [mail] couriers leave on Tuesdays and Fridays.

Wednesday. 19 June. Boating exercises were in the morning. I read and worked. After breakfast everyone went ashore, but I remained with Mama. She was lying down on the deck. N.P sat nearby. I read and talked to Rodionov, who was on watch duty. Ocassionally it rained heavily but it was warm and the sun came out for a bit. Before dinner I played "buno" with Pavl. Al. and Nastenka, fun. Mama went downstairs after 9 o'cl. Papa played kosti. Aunt Olga went to a picnic. I sat with N.P. in Mama's cabin. 37 [degrees] because of the heart, No.2. [It was] 16 degrees in the evening after the flag ceremony.

Thursday. 20 June. Did not do anything in the morning. There were boating exercises. Papa kayaked. Cutter-gig[169] escort (Pavl. Al.). Very warm and nice, sunny. At 2 o'cl. [it was] 34 degrees in the sun on quarterdeck. In the afternoon [we] went ashore. Played 6 sets with Rodionov against Papa and Anya. Won 2 of them, and lost 4. Returned at 5 1/2. Some dog swam to the front gangway. They

---

[168] Card game

[169] A ship's boat between a cutter and a gig in build and size.

took him into a motorboat to look for the ship she came from. Turned out, he [sic] was from "The Kazanetz". Mama came out for dinner, but returned to her cabin at 10 o'cl. I think she does not feel well, but she is not saying anything. After dinner T and I went to the control room. Dear Pavl. Al. was writing in the log journal. We sat together until 10 o'cl. Then Aunt Olga left, and we sat and had tea with N.P. 15 degrees. Beautiful sunset, very quiet.

Friday. 21 June. Had boating exercises in the morning as usual. [I] read and then sat on the afterdeck with Pavl. Al. for a long while. It was so nice. At breakfast and dinner [I] sat with N.P. In the afternoon [we] went to play tennis. I played 2 sets with Aunt Olga against A and Baron [von] Nolde and lost miserably. Very warm. [We] baked in the sun. Baron N. was teaching me to walk on stilts. After that I did the giant steps with him. Papa played with Anya, Khvoshinsky, and Rodionov. Then everyone went swimming but returned to the yacht. After tea I read on deck with T. Pavl. Al. came at 7 o'cl, and we sat together until 7 1/2. Went to moleben. Mama went downstairs at 10 1/2, heart 2. It was very funny to watch A talk to Pavl. Al. through the half port on afterdeck. Until 11 ½ [we] sat there with him. Aunt Olga left for the ""Polar Star" at 10 1/2. Papa played kosti. 15 1/2 degrees in the evening. Did not get to say good night to N.P.

"After tea I read on deck..." Olga reading, Anastasia sitting next to her

Saturday. 22 June. There were boating exercises even though it was Saturday. Papa kayaked. A tent was set up. In the afternoon [we] went ashore. Played one set with Pavl. Al. against Papa and Aunt Olga. We earned 8 [points], they – 6. Then played another one with B. Nolde against them and T, Sh. Semyonov. Baked in the sun, played on giant steps. Papa and the officers went swimming. We returned to the yacht. Vsenoshnaya was held on the afterdeck. Mama left the deck at about 11 o'cl. She is tired, but I don't know how she is feeling, she looks pale. In the evening [I] stayed in the front control room with dear Pavl. Al.

Rodionov is on watch duty, filling in for Butykov who is still sick. It was warm and cozy. Anya has tonsillitis. My throat is also a little sore. Aunt Olga stayed until 10 1/2. Papa played kosti. Again I did not have a chance to wish N.P. good night.

"Baked in the sun." Olga and her sisters loved to lie out in the sun. Anastasia is smoking in this photo.

Sunday. 23 June. Obednya was held on afterdeck at 10 1/2. Then we had a big breakfast. In the afternoon everyone went ashore. I remained behind on watch duty. First I read on deck, then sat in front control room with Pavl. Al., Rodionov and Sablin. Mama was downstairs initially. N.P. was hanging up paintings for her. Then she was lying down on the quarterdeck starboard. At 6 ½ we 4 and Papa went to Padio. Some of the crew members from our yacht and "The Polar Star" were on shore. The officers and Aunt Olga were also there. We walked through the woods for ¼ an hour and finally came to the picnic site. [They] set up a stage there, and a few people from The Polar Star performed 2 plays. Very funny. We all sat on the rocks. After that there was dancing, first to an accordion, then musicians played. Lots of Finns came over from the villages with little children. The crew had a lot fun and danced a lot. [We] went to dinner at 9 o'cl. Sat at the table until 11 o'cl. because by the end of dinner the singers came out, and they sang and danced and every other thing one can imagine. Artemiev and T.[atiana] Yevg.[enievna] were really making everyone laugh on stage. They told funny stories on stage and mimicked sailors from different countries, danced folk dances in different [ways], the way they dance them in various provinces. Then we returned to the old spot and danced again. We danced with the officers. Then Allaverdov, etc. Datzoev danced the "lezginka"[170] very well and did not even get tired. When he finished, Artemiev started mimicking him – [it was] unbelievably funny. The last dance was the polonaise to the "Old Ranger" march. I danced with Pavl. Al. [We] returned to the yacht at 12 o'cl 35 min. Mama was already in bed. It was so nice and fun.

---

[170] National dance from the Caucasus Mountains

Olga and her sisters in the woods in Finland

Monday. 24 June. Papa went kayaking. They had boating exercises. At breakfast [I] sat with N.P., then went to play tennis. Played 2 sets with Aunt Olga against T and Baron Nalde. We won the first one but lost the other one. Then we just sat on the grass. Aunt Olga slept. Papa played with Pavlov against Pavl. Al and Kvoshinsky. Then we played giant steps, went swimming and then returned to the yacht. Mama's heart is No.2. Sat on the deck before dinner. In the evening Kozhevnikov, Pavl. Al. and Rodionov received supplies– 22 tons. In the morning a deck tent was set up. Mama went downstairs at about 10 o'cl. 45 min. Anya is still in bed. Papa read in his cabin downstairs. I sat with Mama and N.P., it was fun, we laughed a lot. Aunt Olga, T, Rodionov and Zlebov were on the upper

deck bridge. At 10 1/2 Aunt Olga went to the P[olar] S[tar]. We stayed on deck

until 11 o'cl. 12 min. Dear Pavl. Al. was on watch duty. I stayed with him when he

was not busy. Rodionov was in the saloon. The new mechanic Ippolit

Mikhailovich Mochalov played the piano. At 8 o'cl. "The Neva" yacht arrived. […]

with 5 mine layers. "The Minin", "The Amur", "The Yenisey", "The Volga" and

"The Onega" dropped anchors to dock in the large harbor.

Olga and "Pavl. Al." (Pavel Voronov, right). Nicholas and another officer are in background

Tuesday. 25 June. Naryshkin and Arseniev left today. Count Grabbe and

Drenteln arrived in their places. Papa went to review the vessels. Went into the sea on "The Pogranichnik", where they installed the mines. All the commanders and 2 admirals had breakfast with us. In the afternoon [we] went ashore. [We] played 2 sets with Papa against Rodionov and T. We won one set, but lost the other. Then I played 2 more with Rodionov against Papa and Zelenetzky. Won 1, lost 1. Everyone went swimming, returned for tea. [It was] rather overcast but warm. 15 degrees in the evening. Mama is still not feeling well. Temperature 37.2, and she went to bed early. Before dinner I read in the control room. Pavl. Al. was on watch duty. After dinner and until 10 o'clock [we] were on upper deck bridge. Pavl. Al. wrote in the journal. Aunt Olga, Rodionov, Zlebov, Mochalov were also there. Count Maklakov arrived on "The Don Cossack" with a report. He left after 9 o'cl. In the evening they showed a cinematograph in the dining room – our whole trip[171]. [I] saw AKSHV from far away in Moscow and Yaroslavl[172]. Went to bed at 11 o'cl. 50 min. Sat with N.P. at dinner.

---

[171] She probably means the newsreel footage of their tercentenary procession.

[172] Presumably in the film footage.

"We laughed a lot". Olga's charming smile

Wednesday. 26 June. Boating exercises. Papa kayaked, I read. In the afternoon [we] went to play tennis. Played 2 sets with Rodionov against Papa and Aunt Olga. We won both. Played 1 set with Papa – we lost. [It was] so nice in the sun. Everyone went swimming. Mama was lying down on quarterdeck portside. Heart No.2. Windy. At 6 1/2 "The Turkmenetz of Stavropol" arrived with Nastenka. In the evening they showed a cinematograph to the crew, and we watched too. [I] sat next to dear Pavl. Al. the entire time. [I] love him so much. Before that [I] went into the saloon with Aunt Olga. Mochalov played the piano. Everything ended at 11 o'cl. 2 min, and we went downstairs. Papa played kosti. It is 19 degrees in my cabin.

Thursday. 27 June. Went to the flag ceremony for the first time this year. At 8 o'cl. 15 min., Papa, Aunt Olga and the officers took "The Razvedchik", which was docked at port, at the quarry. From there they walked 15 miles to the telegraph, went swimming and came back for breakfast. I sat on the deck, read. The deck tent was set up: starboard 23, portside 20. [They] held boating exercises. Pavl. Al. is on watch duty. Sat with N.P. at breakfast. In the afternoon everyone went ashore. I remained with Mama. She was lying down on quarterdeck starboard, [was] very tired. Stayed there until 10 o'cl. [It was] windy and hot, 20 degrees inside the cabin. Poor Mama's heart is 2 and constant backache, does not stop for a minute. May the Lord save her. N.P. also sat there. Anya came out. After 6 o'cl. I read on deck. When Pavl. Al. came, we went to the top control room, where he was filling in the log journal, and I was dictating. Sat there together until 7 o'cl. Then he went to the saloon for dinner, not with us, since he had to write down the interrogation. Received cargo. Kokovtsov arrived on "Roksana" with a report for Papa. Aunt Olga left – [it was]so sad. Tomorrow at 6 in the morning they are leaving for Kronshtadt. In the evening sat with Pavl. Al. (so nice) and

165

Rodionov between telegraph room and chimney. Migalov was there too. Mama left early. Papa read in his cabin downstairs. Beautiful sunset.

"I read on deck." Olga was an avid reader.

Friday. 28 June. Boating exercises. Deck tent was set up. "The Vodoley No.2" came up. At 12 o'cl. they held a panikhida on afterdeck. Today is the anniversary of Uncle Georgi's[173] death. Neither violins nor balalaikas were

---

[173] Grand Duke Georgi was Nicholas II's younger brother, who died of a chronic illness in 1899 at age 28.

played. Very warm. Played tennis with Papa against Pavl. Al. and Poups (Pototsky). We won 1 set, they won 2. Everyone went swimming, but we returned [to the yacht]. Papa, Pokrovsky, Gr.-Gr. and Zlebov kayaked. They got soaked by the waves. At a little past 6 o'cl. saw Pavl. Al. walking to the top deck bridge and of course [I] followed him. I dictated the log journal to him, after that we sat on the sofa cozily and chatted. He is so considerate. At half past 7 [I] got dressed for dinner. Sat with N.P. Molebna was held. Did not do anything in the evening because Pavl. Al. went to bed, since he has watch duty. Mama did not come out in the evening, does not feel well, her heart still aches, temperature 37.7. At 11 o'cl .15 min. Papa went to Peterhof on "The Tsarevna", to the Yerivansky regiment parade. Of course, it is difficult for her, the darling. May the Lord save her.

Olga and Pavel Voronov on deck

Saturday. 29 June. The weather is very warm although windy as usual. It is 20 degrees in my cabin at 11 o'cl. 20 min. [I] read in the morning. The deck and the board were being washed, the water was pumped out. It was so nerve-wrecking to be at breakfast without Papa and to thank the musicians. [We] went ashore at 2 o'cl. 15 min. as usual. Played 7 sets with Pavl. Al. Won only 1 set, because T and Rodionov played well, but I stank. Papa came on "The Ukraine" – 24 knots –

[it] swayed all of us. "The Polar Star" also arrived. Vsenoshnaya was held on afterdeck. Mama did not come out all day. Heart 2 and [illeg – headache?]. Played in the saloon. Dear Pavl. Al. is on watch duty, it was so nice. Papa played kosti. I stared at Pavl. Al. from the half-port. Beautiful evening.

Sunday. 30 June. Obednya was held at 10 ½ on afterdeck as usual. Mama did not get up all day. In the evening her heart was 2, temperature 37.4, pulse 100. Still not good at all, [it is] sad. In the afternoon [we] went ashore. Played 3 sets with Khvoshinsky against Papa and Rodionov. We won 2, they – 1. Then we stretched out on the grass with Drenteln, Gr. Gr., Mochalov and Baron Nalde. Did not do anything before dinner. Walked and sat with Pavl. Al., he is on watch duty from 4 until 8 o'cl. Did not see N.P. in the evening. Sat with T, Pavl. Al. and Mochalov on upper deck bridge. At first he wrote in the log journal, then we just sat. Initially it was fun but then sadness set in. It got cold, and I felt weak for some reason, foolish. Papa played kosti. In the afternoon it was windy but warm.

July

Monday. 1 July. Bekker arrived yesterday, which was why I stayed in bed [and] read until breakfast. Everyone went ashore. I remained with Mama. She was in bed. It was dark in her cabin. Her heart is over 2, difficult to breathe, headache, backache, legs and arms – not good at all. [I] sat with her. After 4 o'cl. [I] dictated the log journal to Pavl. Al. on deck. Suddenly a heavy rain and strong surf started. Did not do anything after tea. Read in the saloon and talked to Pavl. Al. In the evening Mama went to [lie down on] her sofa. N.P. went to [see] her because it was getting boring. Sat with Pavl. Al. between telegraph control room and chimney. Rodionov stopped by during watch duty. T talked to him. Then Mochalov came. Papa played kosti. Went to bed at 11 o'cl.

Tuesday. 2 July. Stayed in bed half of the morning. Went to play tennis in the afternoon. Bowled with Nastenka, Drenteln, Mochalov and Sablin. It was boring. Did not get a chance to sit with Pavl. Al. I was lying on the grass. Papa played with Poupse, Rodionov and Melnitzky (from "The Turkmenetz"). After tea sat with Pavl. Al. in the control room and dictated the log journal to him. It was nice to sit on the sofa with him. Right before dinner strong wind and very heavy rain started, but it soon subsided. In the afternoon Mama was lying down on the quarterdeck. She did not come out in the evening. She feels a little better but not much. In the evening stayed on deck with N.P., then he, I, Nastenka, Pavl. Al., Rodionov and

Kozhevnikov played different card games in our control room. It was lots of fun. Papa played kosti with Zelenetzky, Zlebov and Drenteln.

"Went to play tennis..." Olga, Anastasia and Tatiana (lying down) on a tennis court

Wednesday. 3 July. The sisters went swimming. I remained on the yacht. Papa went kayaking. [They] had boating exercises. In the afternoon [we] went to play tennis. Papa played with M against T and Pavl. Al. I sat on the grass. After that [I]

bowled with Pavl. Al., M and Sablin. Picked wild strawberries. In the afternoon Mama was lying down on the quarter-deck and did not get up in the evening. Heart is not good again and aches, as well as [her] left arm. Dinner was at 7 1/2. At 9 o'cl. the yacht sailed off and went to Revel. Beautiful weather, no wind at all. 16 degrees on quarterdeck. [There was] a lot of soot - the smoke was rising. At first I sat with dear Pavl. Al. between telegraph control room and chimney on the disassembled gangway. Then he went to bed since he has watch duty. Had tea at 11 o'cl, walked around and sat with Rodionov and T. N.P. went to [see] Mama. I sat with him at breakfast.

Thursday. 4 July. Between Revel and Hogland[174]. Horn sounds woke me up at 5 1/2. Thick fog. [We] dropped anchor about 3 miles away from Revel. T and I kept looking out through the half-ports. At 8 o'cl [we] went out on deck for the flag ceremony and then entered the port. Around 9 o'cl. Papa went out to sea aboard "The Rurik" to shoot against the Baltic Fleet[175]. Returned late, had a big breakfast, which ended at 3 o'cl. After that Papa visited 2 ships. I sat in the control room, did not read much, talked to Pavl. Al. instead. Papa returned at 5 1/2. We raised the anchor and returned. The entire fleet escorted us to Kok-skerries where we raised the banner and all the ships saluted. After that we returned to Revel. Played with Pavl. Al., Rodionov and Nastenka until 7 o'cl. on the afterdeck. After that [we] sat on the stern and talked. There were two gales with torrential rain during dinner. Warm. Sat in control [room] by the window, read

---

[174] A rocky island in the Gulf of Finland.

[175] Presumably shooting exercises

and stared at dear Pavl. Al., who kept watch duty on deck bridge. Then walked around the wet deck with T and Sablin. At about 11 o'cl. went to see Mama. N.P. was there. Papa read in his cabin. She was lying down on quarterdeck portside by the control room. A giant tent was set up in the morning.

Friday. 5 July. Dropped anchor at about 4 o'cl in the morning. Beautiful weather. Deck tent was set up. Papa kayaked, escorted by the cutter-gig. In the afternoon [we] went to play tennis. I played 2 sets with Rodionov against Anya and Butakov, won both. Then I walked around on stilts, sat, then played 2 more sets with Khvoshinsky (Mishka) against Papa and Butakov. We won one set, but lost the other. Mama was lying down on the quarterdeck starboard. After tea and until 7 ½ [I] sat on deck by front right gangway with Pavl. Al. He was on watch duty with Rodionov, Mishka and T.Sh. Semyonov. 2nd team went to unload the coal on The Polezny. Moleben was at 8 as usual. After dinner [I] sat in the control room with Pavl. Al. and T. He was filling out the log journal. After that sat on the quarterdeck portside with him, Rodionov, Ippolit and Nastenka and played a game similar to Flower Dallying. After that played Affections with dear sweet Pavl. Al. and it turned out well. Went to bed at 11.35. It was cozy and unreasonably great to be with him. Mama did not come out. [Her] heart aches, No.2. N.P. went to [see] her. Papa played kosti. It is 19 degrees in my cabin. Thank God for everything.

"...[I] sat on deck by the front right gangway with Pavl. Al." Olga with Pavel Voronov.
Maria is standing in background on the right.

Saturday. 6 July. The sisters went ashore to swim. Papa kayaked. I sat on the

deck and in Mama's cabin, read. Did not go ashore in the afternoon, remained

behind on [watch] duty. Mama was lying down on quarterdeck starboard. N.P.

pasted in the album for her. I [sat] between them and Pavl. Al. (on watch duty).

174

When his shift was over at 4, I dictated the log journal to him. After that we sat on the sofa until after 5 o'cl. I love him, the dear one, so much. At 7 o'cl vsenoshnaya was held on afterdeck. After dinner we 3 played cards on the quarterdeck (portside) with Pavl. Al, Nastenka, Kozhevnikov and Gr. Gr. It was nice, but sad for some reason. A[nastasia] went to bed early. She was horsing around a lot with Pavl. Al. and Zlebov until 10 o'cl. Everyone is teasing her for being short, and she gets angry. Papa played kosti as always. Mama did not come upstairs: 37.5 and fast pulse. May the Lord save her. Accepted "The Vodoley No.2" [...] 16 degrees inside the tent. About 20 degrees in the cabin. [I] wonder what AKSHV is doing. Have not seen him for a month already.

Olga and Tatiana with officers

175

Sunday. 7 July. Obednya was held on the afterdeck as usual. Then Papa reviewed the crew and we had a big breakfast. In the afternoon [we] went ashore. I played 2 sets with Pavl. Al. against Poupse and Anya, and we lost both. Then played 2 more sets with Mishka against Papa and Anya, and we won both. It was hot on the beach. Between games we took breaks on the grass. After 6 o'cl. Tatiana and I sat in control room with Pavl. Al. He was filling in the log journal. I love being with him so much. In the evening Mama finally came up to the deck. Pavl. Al., Rodionov, Ippolit, Nastenka and I played cards by her side. N.P. and Anya sat with Mama. Papa played kosti as usual. Beautiful evening. It is 20 degrees inside the cabin. The tent was up all day. Pavl. Al. seemed a bit sad. He enjoyed himself just a little today, as he showed me just the tip of his pinky.

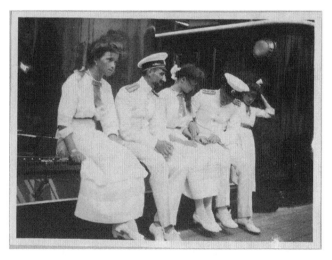

Olga, Pavel Voronov, Tatiana, another officer and Anastasia on deck of the yacht

176

Monday. 8 July. At 9 Papa took T and me on "The Turkmenetz of Stavropol". Papa inspected it, and then we went into a big bay, where they demonstrated mine-sweeping maneuvers with "The Steregushy". It was very interesting. Went to Pukion-sari and back. A few of Papa's officers were there. Pavl. Al. was also there, as well as the commander of "The Vesyoly". Then [we] went to "The Ukraine". – Polushkin. Then – on No.218 – [...], No.219 – Kryzhanovsky. They stood together, the latter was inspecting The Steregushy. Returned at 11 1/2. In the afternoon played tennis: 3 sets with Papa against T and Mishka. We won only one game, it was very hot in the sun. I read and wrote letters in my cabin until dinner. In the evening [they] showed a cinematograph to the crew. We also watched. They showed funny motion pictures. I sat with dear Pavl. Al. on the bench. It was so nice! Mama was lying down by the control room. N.P. was with her. In the afternoon [it was] 22 degrees in the tent. 21 degrees in my cabin. Beautiful evening. It rained suddenly, then cleared up.

Tuesday. 9 July. At 9 o'cl. Papa and we 4 went on "The Kazanetz", inspected it, then went on "The Strashny"[176]. Went to sea at 24 knots, very nice. The ship was rocking. It was nice to be on the bow – we got sprayed with water a lot and sprinkled with soot. The commander of The K[azanetz] is Dmitriev, the commander of The S[trashny] – Zarubaev, both [were] decorated with the St George's crosses. In the afternoon played tennis with Khvoshinsky against Papa and T. and won all 3 games. Very warm and windy, [we] were lying on the grass.

[176] "The Kazanetz" and "The Strashny" are names of two ships

Did not do anything after tea. Sat in my cabin and in the control room. Pavl. Al. went to dinner. He starts [his] watch duty at 8 o'cl. I feel lonesome without him. The Vodolei No.2 came to unload cargo. The moon came out, [it was] very quiet. In the evening Nastenka, Rodionov, Ippolit and I played cards and geography on the deck. Mama was lying down nearby. N.P. was there. Her heart is beating fast and hard. Papa played kosti. 20 1/2 degrees in the cabin.

"We two"

Wednesday. 10 July. Papa went to [inspect] 2 vessels in the morning. At 10 ocl. 35 min. we went ashore to swim. [It was] so nice in the water. Before that, [I] sat in the control room with Pavl. Al. Rodionov stood by the window. When we

178

returned to the yacht, Papa went [swimming?]. I played tennis with T. against Nastenka and Anya, and we lost miserably, did not make a single score in one set. After that went back to the yacht and sat in the cabin. I felt lonesome without Pavl. Al., but he is on watch duty from 4 o'clock. At 7 1/2 Papa and Aleksei worked with the musicians. After dinner A and I went to the control room. I dictated the log journal to Pavl. Al. Then [I] played lotto with him in the saloon. It was so cozy. Sat with N.P. Mama was also there. [It was] very warm, the moon, quiet. 21 1/2 degrees in my cabin. Got a nice gift from Papa and Mama with a sapphire and a brooch.

"I played tennis with T. against Nastenka and Anya..." Left to right: Maria, Tatiana, an officer, Olga and Anastasia. Vyrubova is standing behind them.

Thursday. 11 July. Received lovely bouquets of white roses from our yacht, from "The Tsarevna", "The Polar Star", "The Ukraine", from the fleet captain and the entire crew. All commanders had breakfast for the last time. There was obednya on the after-deck at noon. Pavl. Al. was on watch duty. In the morning Papa kayaked, the sisters went swimming, but I stayed with Mama in her cabin. In the afternoon everyone went to play tennis, but I remained behind. Until 4 o'cl. Mama was in her cabin with N.P. I read on the deck. A little after 4 o'cl., when Pavl. Al.'s shift was over, I dictated the log journal to him. A few minutes later everyone returned from the shore, and I went to Mama's, who came out on the quarter-deck portside. Suddenly it started to rain heavily with wind gusts and thunderstorm. During breakfast two masts[?] broke. After 6 o'cl. we 4 stopped by N.P.'s cabin, because M and A needed to sign something. [We] stayed with the officers in the saloon for a bit, and then went to get changed for dinner. After molebna we took group pictures as we do every year. Did not do anything in the evening, just sat by the kitchen on the left with dear N.P., Rodionov and Mochalov. Then Nastenka came over. Nice evening, warm. Went to bed at 11 ocl. 45 min. 19 1/2 degrees in the cabin. So sad – it's [our] last night. I got 44 telegrams.

"After molebna we took group pictures as we do every year".

Friday. 12 July. Peterhof. Got up in time for the flag ceremony, "Moscow-Paris" and another march was playing. Pavl. Al. was on watch duty from 8 o'clock. Papa swam for the last time from starboard front gangway. At 10 o'cl. [we] went to sea. Lowered the speed twice because the bearings overheated. Wonderful sea, sun, the weather [was] warm. I was sitting on the foredeck [and] looking at the deck-bridge, etc. Mama came upstairs before breakfast. [I] sat in the control room with Pavl. Al., the sisters, Ippolit and Rodionov until our arrival in Kronshtadt at 3 o'cl. It was awfully sad. I stood with him the entire time the gangway was extended. [We] left the yacht at about 4 o'clock. [It] was so awfully hard to part with the beloved Standart, the officers and the beloved [last word was crossed out, probably by Olga]. May the Lord keep him, everyone and N.P. Went to Peterhof aboard "The Alexandria". Had tea and dinner with Papa and Mama. So sad to be without them. The yacht followed us to Petersburg, we watched it depart. It saluted as [it was] leaving Kronshtadt. In the evening sat with Papa and Mama. [Her] headache is better but she is tired.

13 July. Saturday. At 10 1/2 T and I rode on horseback. I rode Regent. We went to the lower park, the English park and the large training ground, [we] were learning to make an entrance with Korzhavin[177]. Warm, sunny, windy. Had breakfast with Papa and Count Fredericks, Mama was in her study. In the afternoon [we] played tennis with Papa and Nastenka. I thought about the past, about my darling, it's so sad without him and the others. Had tea and dinner with Papa and Mama. In the evening talked to N.P. and Ippolit on the telephone. Mama's heart is almost 3, [she] does not feel well. Went to vsenoshnaya.

Sunday. 14 July. Before obednya [I] talked on the telephone with N.P., Rodionov and The Sweet One. He is on watch duty. It was so nice. There was a big breakfast at the farm. In the afternoon [we] played tennis with Anya against Papa and T, and lost. Then Rodionov came over, and T played with him against me and Papa. They won 2 sets, we won 1. It's cool, sunny and windy today. We rode [our] bicycles there. Had tea and dinner with Papa and Mama. Mama did not come down today. Heart was 2 in the morning, 1 ½ in the evening, she is tired and still has a headache. She does not look good. Again talked on the telephone

---

[177] Possibly a riding instructor

with N.P., heard the "Moscow" march in the background, and all the good memories returned. 7 degrees in the evening. Went to bed at 11 o'cl.

"In the afternoon [we] played tennis with Anya against Papa and T, and lost." Tatiana, Anastasia, Nicholas and Olga on tennis court with some officers

Monday. 15 July. Got up early and waited for the yacht to pass by. When it did pass at about 9 o'cl. we waved to it, and they saluted. Strong wind, chilly. Rode horses with T, I rode Korbo (the black horse). Had breakfast, tea and dinner with Papa and Mama upstairs. In the afternoon played tennis with Papa, Anya and the sisters. Mama did not come down today. She aches all over and her heart is enlarged. Heard [music?] play in the distance. Wonder what The Sweet One is doing. May the Lord keep them all. 7 degrees. Papa and Mama received a telegram from the commanders. They went by Hogland at 3.40.

Tuesday. 16 July. Went to Mikhailovka on horseback. I rode Regent. Had breakfast, tea and dinner with Papa and Mama upstairs. Played tennis with Papa, Nastenka, Poupse and Semyonov. Played lots of sets. It was nice, reminded [me] of the holiday. Windy, a bit of water. Good news from the yacht: 5 ball seas, chilly, passed Hogland. Mama's heart was 2 in the evening. Aleksei's right arm hurts, he is crying. Mama sat with him and was lying down in the small room. 10 degrees. Went to bed at 10 1/2.

Wednesday. 17 July. Rode on horseback. I rode Regent. Had breakfast with Papa and Mitya Dehn. In the afternoon played tennis with him, Anya and Nastenka. Warmer, the wind subsided. Had tea and dinner with Papa. Mama was in bed all day. Aleksei stayed with her while his arm hurts, poor thing. Grigori Yef[imovich] came over. In the evening sat with Papa, Mama and Anya. 11 degrees in the evening. Mama had a headache ever since we returned. Temperature 37.4, pulse 95. She is tired. The yacht left the Kilsky canal.

Thursday. 18 July. We 2 walked to Aunt Ella's farm, then had lessons. Had breakfast with Papa, Aunt Ella and Uncle Nikolai[178]. In the afternoon Mama and Aleksei were lying down on the balcony in the sun – [it was] warm. Played tennis with Papa, Anya, Mishka and Semyonov. Good news from the yacht – they are in

---

[178] H.I.H. Grand Duke Nikolai Nikolaevich of Russia

the German sea. Had tea on the balcony. Had dinner with Papa, Aunt and Dmitri. After that sat with Mama upstairs. Went to bed at about 11 o'cl. 11 degrees.

"We 2..."

Friday. 19 July. Rode Regent. It's finally very warm today. Had breakfast and dinner with Papa and the Aunt. Played tennis with Papa. Anya came over later. Had tea on the balcony. Mama and Aleksei were lying down. At 6 o'cl. Sofia Iv[anovna] Tyutcheva[179] came over. We sat on the balcony in the sun. After dinner sat with Mama and the Aunt. Papa read. It has been a week since we are back, sad. The yacht arrived in Portsmouth. 12 degrees.

---

[179] One of the grand duchesses' former governesses

Saturday. 20 July. Rode on Regent. Papa went to the 100th anniversary parade of the 14th Yeniseisky regiment. Had breakfast with Aunt Ella. After that dyed scarves on the balcony with her and Mama. Aleksei is feeling better, thank God. He was there too. Then [we] played tennis with Papa and Anya. Had tea with Papa, Mama and Aunt Ella. Mama had dinner in her [room], we had dinner downstairs. Went to vsenoshnaya. 12 degrees, warm. It was windy in the afternoon, but calm in the evening.

Sunday. 21 July. At 9.20 Aunt Irene[180] arrived. Papa, T and I went to meet her and took her to the farm. Went to obednya. Had breakfast and dinner with both Aunts and Papa. Had tea with them and Mama. Aleksei got dressed. At 11 the yacht left Portsmouth. In the afternoon took a boat ride with M and A and 2 sailors. Papa and T went kayaking. Then [we] walked with Papa and did giant steps. In the evening worked upstairs at Mama's. Temperature 37.4. She is tired, but [looks] beautiful. 14 degrees in the evening.

---

[180] Empress Alexandra's sister and wife of Prince Heinrich of Prussia, younger brother of Kaiser Wilhelm II.

Olga, Tatiana and Anastasia with their father, governesses and some officers. It looks like Olga (far right) may be smoking a cigarette.

Monday. 22 July. Obednya was held at 11 o'cl. There were a lot of people, a big breakfast was served. [It was] very hot in the sun. Musicians of the guard played. Good news from the yacht, thank God. In the afternoon [I] played tennis with Papa, Anya, Mishka and Semyonov. Had tea with Papa, Mama and both Aunts. Had dinner without Mama, she stayed upstairs, her heart was No.2 in the evening. After dinner we 2 and Papa went to the small pier and rode on The Bunchuk around "The Ukraina" and around "The Tsarevna", [it was] such a nice, lovely evening. At 11 o'cl. saw Aunt Ella off. She is going to The Solovky Monastery[181]. [...]

Tuesday. 23 July. At 9 ocl. 45 min T, Aunt Irene and I went to Tsarskoe Selo in a motor. Chief lady-in waiting Lori Yertsen went too. [We] inspected the regimental church and the Grand Palace. After that [we] went to [see] Aunt Miechen. Sat in her garden. Later Uncle Kyrill and Aunt Ducky came over. Returned for breakfast. Uncle Andrei came over. In the afternoon we 5 dyed scarves downstairs on the balcony with Mama and the Aunt. Had tea and dinner with them. Papa went to Krasnoe Selo for camp inspection, a wrap-up, dinner and a theater performance. We all sat on the balcony and worked. There were so many flies, awful. No news from the yacht. 13 degrees. The sky is overcast, it drizzled.

---

[181] Also known as "Solovetsky Monastery": founded in the 15th century, the monastery later served as a place of exile for opponents of Autocracy and Orthodoxy. After the revolution it became a prison camp and the prototype of Gulag.

Olga and Tatiana with their Aunt Irene.

Wednesday. 24 July. At 10 o'cl. 20 min T, Papa and I went to Kronshtadt on The

Alexandria. [It was] chilly and windy. Admiral Makarov's monument was beautiful.

There was moleben and a parade. Had breakfast on the way back. Saw a lot of

old acquaintances. In the afternoon played tennis with Papa, Mishka, Count

Nalde and Anya. It was fun. Had tea with Papa, Mama and the Aunt. Papa had dinner with the Greeks[182]. We had dinner upstairs with Mama, Dmitri and Aunt. After 6 o'cl. A and I rode bicycles to Derevenko's house, where we played with his son and my godson Evegeny (Varvara's son). They are so sweet. Worked in the afternoon.

Olga with Maria and Anastasia

---

[182] The Greek royal family

Thursday. 25 July. At 10 o'cl. we 2 and Aunt[183] went to Krasnoe Selo. We watched the parade in the military field from the imperial podium with the other relatives. It was very nice. Finally saw my regiment. It marched brilliantly of course, as did the Yerivansky regiment. Saw B.-B., but he was not on horseback due to broken arm. AKSHV was there. Today is his birthday. After the parade [we] had breakfast there and then went to show houses to Aunt with Papa. We came back at 2 o'cl., but Papa remained for the races, dinner with the heavy cavalry regiment and theater. We sat with Mama, worked and talked. It started raining and is still raining. Chilly, 12 degrees in the evening. Had dinner and tea with Mama and the Aunt. Played cards in the evening. Mama is [feeling] better, thank God. Poor Count Nirod is better. He has [a tumor?] on his liver or kidney, not sure. Still no news from the yacht. I hope everything is going well. During the parade the aeroplanes flew above our heads.

Wednesday. 26 July. At 8 o'cl. saw AKSHV through the window. It was raining, but we two still went to Aunt's and walked with her in wet mud. Had breakfast with her and Papa. At 2 1/2 Papa went to the camp for shooting [practice], etc. We 4 played a lot of tennis. Had tea and dinner with Mama and Aunt. Darling Mama has a severe headache. We all played cards with Aunt and laughed a lot. At about 7 o'cl. We and Aunt went to visit B.M. Talian in Strelna, viewed the gardens. Sunny and chilly. The yacht arrived in Oman for loading. Everything is well, thank God. It is departing for Algiers in the evening.

---

[183] Probably Irene

Saturday. 27 July. Fireworks. We 2 walked around Peterhof with Aunt and Lori Yertsen. They took pictures of the most beautiful sites. Sunny. At 9 1/2 Papa left for maneuvers and returned at 2 o'cl. Had tea with Papa, Mama and the Aunt. Had dinner with Mama and the Aunt. Papa had dinner with the French. [We] played tennis with Anya. It started to rain but then it ended. Went to church. Mama's face aches, but her head[ache] is better. Played cards and smoked.

Sunday. 28 July. At 11 went to obednya. Had breakfast downstairs with Papa and the Aunt. Mama sat on the balcony with Aleksei. Had tea with her there. Played tennis with Papa, Anya, Mishka and the Count. Warm, sunny, cool, fun. The yacht left Algiers. After 6, we four took Aunt to Batligon, the summer cottage, to church and to the pink pavilion. Ran into a sweet old woman and her son, the drunken custodian. Nastasia asked him silly questions. After dinner [we] played cards. Mama and Papa pasted pictures into the album.

"We 2 walked around Peterhof with Aunt and Lori Yertsen."

Monday. 29 July. We four rode horses on training ground, practiced entrance.
When we returned we studied as usual, and Bekker arrived. Had breakfast with
Mama. Aunt is in Petersburg, [she] returned for tea. In the afternoon I sat with
Mama and Anya, worked. Papa went to Krasnoe Selo at 9 1/2, returned in the
evening. Count Nirod is a little better after surgery, thank God. The yacht passed
Bonne in the morning. Mama's cheek is better. She is tired, but better, No.1 in
the evening. After tea we two and Aunt rode in a motor to Sergiyevka, the
English park, etc. Had dinner with her and Mama. In the evening played cards
and looked at sites by Denisov Uralsky. 12 degrees in the evening, sunny, clear,
stars.

Tuesday. 30 July. Went to church late with the Aunt. Big breakfast after moleben. Heavy rain and windy all day. Stayed home with Mama, worked. Had tea and dinner with Mama, Papa and the Aunt. In the evening played cards with the Aunt. Papa and Mama pasted in the album. Aleksei played with paper lanterns with Derevenko's children on the balcony. [I] wrote letters and read. Good news from the yacht – warm, calm seas.

Wednesday. 31 July. Had a music lesson for a ½ hour. At 11 o'cl. 15 min. we two and Nastenka went to Krasnoe Selo for breakfast with the Yerivansky regiment. Also went to [see] their exercises and talked to dear friends Otar, P. Ravtopulo and Prince Eristov, greeted the rest. Before leaving [we] took a group picture in the yard. Around 2 o'cl.went to the military hospital – there were 583 patients. We stopped by all the rooms. At 4 o'cl. [we] went to the military field where Tatiana's and my regiments had exercises. It was very nice. I was so happy to have a close look at the regiment. Foggy, damp, rainy. At 7 o'cl. had dinner with our officers. All the commanders introduced themselves. The Aunt, M and A came to the field. Returned home a little after 9 o'cl. Sat with Mama and played cards with her and the Aunt. Papa went to the theater.

~

August

Olga and Tatiana

Thursday. 1 August. At about 1 o'cl. [I] sat in Mama's bedroom and held a heating pad on Aleksei's right arm. It hurts again. Had lessons. Had breakfast with Papa, the Aunt, Lori Yertsen and the Khan. In the afternoon visited an engraving factory with Papa and the Aunt. Rain, damp, chilly. Had tea and dinner with Papa, Mama and the Aunt. In the evening played cards. A telegram came at 5 o'cl. in the morningt: the yacht had entered the Dardanelles. May the Lord save us. During dinner, Mama's face ached a lot. Poor Count Nirod is still not feeling well. Temperature 38 in the evening.

Friday. 2 August. We 2 and Aunt rode on horseback to the military training field and practiced entering with the 1st Kuban half-Hundred. Zhukov, Veter, Gulyga and Sklerov. Had breakfast with Mama and the Aunt. Had tea and dinner with them and with Papa, who went to the maneuvers at 9 1/2 and returned. Played tennis with Papa, Anya and Mishka. Sunny. After tea we put on our uniforms and tried riding horses around the garden. I rode Korbo and Regent. T – Yarka and Robino. At 7 o'cl. the yacht safely arrived in Sevastopol. Thank God. Everyone played cards. Mama's cheek hurts. Aleksei is a lot better, he was lying down on the balcony in a cheerful mood.

Saturday. 3 August. Rode on horseback with T, A and the Aunt. Practice on the training grounds again with the 3rd Terskaya Hundred: Dolgov, Tatonov and Zershikov. I rode Regent and Korbo. Had breakfast with Papa, Aunts Irene, Miechen and Ducky, and Uncle Kyrill. Mama stayed in her [room]. Aleksei is better, he got dressed today. At 3 1/2 Papa, Aunt and we went to the military field, where we watched the cavalry exercises and maneuvers. Papa was on

196

horseback. It was long but interesting. B.-B. was there. I saw my regiment. Strong wind, dusty, chilly. At 7 o'cl. [we] returned home, had tea. At 8 o'cl. had dinner. Papa stayed. Played cards. Count Nirod is better, thank God. Mama's face still aches.

Sunday. 4 August. Papa went to maneuvers at 8 1/2 and returned at 6 1/2. Went to obednya. Had breakfast and tea with Mama and the Aunt. Had dinner with them and Papa. We four played tennis with Nastenka and Lori Yertsen. Very warm, 15 degrees in the evening. In the morning Count Nirod had a temperature of 39.4, [he was] better in the evening. At 4 o'cl. [we] went to [see] Aunt Mops. Had tea and worked on the balcony. Then rode in a motor with Aunt and saw our dear regiment officers. Played cards.

Monday. 5 August. At 10 o'cl. 35 min. we 2 went to the training grounds in [our] uniforms. Rode on horses: I rode Regent, T - Robino. Uncle Nikolasha[184] rode with me to my regiment. Martynov met me with a report. Then [I] galloped to the trumpet playing, greeted each squadron and met Papa on the right flank. Then I followed him around the front again. I was very nervous about the entrance, but it turned out fine. The parade was nice and beautiful. My wonderful Elizavetgrad regiment marched very well. After breakfast talked on the balcony and took group pictures with Papa and my officers in front of the Grand Palace. Then took pictures with the regimental ladies. It is very sad that Mama could not be here. At

---

[184] Grand Duke Nikolai Nikolaevich, commander-in-chief of the Russian army.

3 1/2 both regiments came over to our garden. Mama was sitting in a wheelchair with Aleksei. The singers sang nice songs as the regiment marched by. Papa and we saw them off to the gate, and the regiment marched past Papa for the last time. The hussars and the officers are so sweet, although I don't know them, but nevertheless. They presented me with a picture album of the best views of the "Olga headquarters". I liked the lieutenant-colonel and Sultan Trei most of all. Had dinner with Mama and the Aunt. Had tea with them, as well as Papa and Dmitri. There was an Austrian dinner. Went to vsenoshnaya. Aunt left at 10, we saw her off to the [train] station. Heard the regimental march and singing from far away – such darlings. They really delighted us. It is very hot today. It was 34 degrees in the sun in the morning at Krasnoe Selo. Poor Count Nirod is in bad shape. Mama's entire face hurts. I am so unbelievably happy with today!!!

"Then [I] galloped to the trumpet playing, greeted each squadron and met Papa at the right flank."
Olga and Tatiana next to their father on horseback, Olga wearing her regiment's Elizavetgrad
Hussar uniform.

Tuesday. 6 August. Poor dear Count Nirod died this morning at 8 o'cl. May God

rest his soul. He suffered awfully last night, but was surprisingly patient. His poor

widow and his mother, who lost her third son, and her fourth son is dying from

tuberculosis. Terribly sad. Went to obednya. It was raining. The sun came out in

the afternoon, and it became almost hot. Had dinner with Mama and Nastenka.

Went with her and T to [see] her mother in Strelna. After we returned, went with Papa on "The Alexandria" and "The Rabotnik". Papa thanked the crew for their service. Had tea with Papa and Mama on the balcony. At 6 o'cl. Grigory Yefimovich came over. Papa made a 2nd trip to Krasnoe Selo. In the morning he went to the Preobrazhensky regiment parade, then returned home and read in his [room]. Then went back there for dinner. He went to a molebna. I sat with Mama and Anya.

On the train. Wednesday. 7 August. Did not do anything all morning. Maria has high fever, a stomach ache, she had diarrhea (about 30 times a day). At 10 o'cl. 45 min. a molebna was held. We left at 12 o'cl. A lot of people were there to see us off as usual. I was happy to leave. In the afternoon [I] stayed with Mama, read. She was lying down with [her] eyes closed. 20 degrees in the shade, very warm. She does not feel well because the train ride is bumpy. In the evening Papa read to us about occasions of awarding the St George's Cross.

Thursday. 8 August. Between Samilov and Pavlograd. Today is poor Count Nirod's funeral – so sad. May the Lord keep us. Did not do anything special in the morning. Sat with Mama, read, made sacks for the bazaar. Aunt Olga got on [our] train in Kursk with the Princess at 2 1/2. It was overcast in the morning, rained at night, was warm in the afternoon. 21 degrees in the shade, sunny. [...]

M is feeling much better. Mama No.3, fair. A moleben and litiya were served in Borki[185]. We are progressing well, thank God. Dusty. I am happy about tomorrow.

Friday. 9 August. The Standart. Sevastopol. Arrived here at 11 1/2. It was very hot and dusty in the train. Mama almost got no sleep, her heart is 2 1/2. So happy to be back on the dear yacht and see everyone. Two of N.P.'s sisters were on the pier. Did not do anything special in the afternoon. Papa went to see the fleet. We two helped The Sweet One write in the log journal after 4 o'cl. and until dinner. Then I sat with him on the deck. It's so nice to be with him, my dear one. Big dinner. In the evening [I] first sat with S.[weet One] by telegraph control room, etc. Then we took a ride in a motor boat around the fleet. There was illumination, but I was bored – I wanted to be with S., had not seen him in so long.

---

[185] In commemoration of the 1888 "Miracle at Borki" (aka the "Borki Disatser") where 23 people were killed and between 12 and 33 injured in a train crash—but the entire Imperial Family was saved.

Olga and Tatiana on the "dear yacht"

Saturday. 10 August. Papa went swimming, but we 3 went into the city with Aunt Olga, N.P., Nevyarovksy and the Princess. We walked along the historic boulevard and the main streets, but crowds followed us everywhere, so we were able to go into only 2 shops for a minute – [it was] very hot. Probably over 30 degrees in the sun. 23 degrees in my cabin. Big breakfast. At 3 ½ we three with Papa and Aunt went in a motor boat to the consecration of a small chapel built in place of old St. Vladimir's church, wrecked during the Sevastopol siege. It was terribly stuffy. Then we inspected the naval hospital and returned. 362 patients.

Before vsenoshnaya everybody was on deck, watching the hydroplanes. In the evening the Aunt, S., Rodionov and we 2 sat between the chimney and control room, played cards with S. and just sat. Papa played kosti. Mama was lying down. N.P. was with her. She was very tired. M is better.

Olga, Maria and Tatiana with Rodionov (left) and Voronov ("S.")

Sunday. 11 August. Went to the Brethren Cemetery[186] for obednya. After that Papa talked to the old invalids. It is very hot today. 40 degrees in the sun on the deck bridge, and strong warm wind. There was a big breakfast and dinner. At 3 1/2 went to Kherson Monastery, watched an archaeological dig. Very interesting, but very hot and dusty. I would have rather stayed on the yacht. After tea, sat with S. on the deck and on foredeck. Others were there, too, listened to the singers, whom he was in charge of, my precious. In the evening sat by the left

---

[186] Mass soldier cemetery

[deck] kitchen with S., Rodionov, T, Aunt Olga and Mityaev. Mama's heart is 2 1/2, still not well. She has trouble breathing outside in the wind. I spent time between her and S. N.P. stopped by too. Papa played kosti. It's 24 1/2 degrees in my cabin. Beautiful night.

Olga, Tatiana and Anastasia with their father at the archaeological dig in Kherson.

Monday. 12 August. At 9 ½ we two and Aunt went swimming to Zimonins in a motor, to [see] the chief commander Admiral Malkovsky. It was very nice in the water – waves and wind. Big breakfast and dinner, as usual. Until 3 1/2 sat on the quarter-deck with S. and Shura, after that went to Balaklava with Papa and the Aunt. There we inspected the new incomplete battery, drank water from St. Georgi the Victor's spring, had tea at Count Apraksin's house with him and his wife. It is delightfully beautiful here. Returned at 7 o'cl. The sailors sang on the front deck. Sat in the saloon with S. and listened to them. In the evening Mama came up on deck for the first time and sat there with N.P. Papa played kosti. [We] stayed by the left [deck] kitchen until 11 o'cl. 45 min. with the Aunt, who was there with Zlebov, Mordvinov and Stolitza. We were there with S. – he is so incredibly nice and affectionate. I love him very, very much. It is almost 24 degrees in my cabin. Very dusty.

Tuesday. 13 August. Swam with Aunt today. The water is a little cooler but very pleasant. Had a big breakfast, the dinner was smaller. S., Rodionov, Aunt and we two sat on the quarter-deck until 3 o'cl., then went in a motor boat to the rocks, and rode in motors along a dusty road to see battlefields, etc. We almost got to Balaklava. It was interesting of course, but I was in a foolish mood, was feeling lonesome because my S. was not there. Returned at 7 o'cl. and sat with S. in the saloon. The singers sang, remarkable job, [they were] the champions (as S. says). After dinner sat with him, Rodionov, the Aunt, Stolitza, Mordvinov and Zlebov until 12 1/2 at night. Oh, [it was] so nice! Mama was lying down and working. Papa and N.P. stayed with her. It was so cozy to sit by the telegraph control room. [We] sipped some kind of drink through a straw.

Wednesday. 14 August. Livadia. Before 10 (when we went out to sea) Papa managed to go to "The Gollandia" to swim with a few officers. Brilliant transfer – banners were raised. The fleet and the batteries saluted. Had breakfast from 11 o'cl. 45 min. until 2, I think, when we arrived in Yalta. I sat in control room with S. The Aunt, the sisters, Shura and Rodionov also came over there. It was sad and hard to part with my S. The honor guard was on the pier, etc. Had tea and dinner and spent the evening on the balcony. I kept looking at the yacht through the fieldglass – saw N.P. and S. 17 degrees in the evening. Went to vsenoshnaya, saw AKSHV. I am happy here but I would have been happier if I remained on the yacht. Mama's face aches again. Tiresome.

Thursday. 15 August. Obednya was held at 11 o'cl. after which – breakfast with the suite. Zlebov, Stolitza, Nevyarovsky and Butakov were invited from the yacht. Saw S. for a moment through the fieldglass. I miss him so much at times, it's awful. In the afternoon walked to Oreanda[187] on the horizontal path with Papa, Aunt and M. Then we returned to the beach and went swimming. So pleasant. Had tea on the balcony. In the evening we 2 played poker with Aunt. Mama worked. Talked to N.P. on the telephone. It rained a little, and we heard far away thunder. Sunny.

---

[187] The Oreanda Palace was built for Empress Alexandra Fedorovna, wife of Emperor Nicholas I, and was began in 1842 by court acrhitect Andrei Stakenschneider. The palace was destroyed by fire in 1882 and never rebuilt, however, the ruins of the two-story neoclassical palace and its formal gardens connected to the Livadia park remained a favorite place for the Imperial Family to walk.

"Had tea on the balcony"

Friday. 16 August. Marie and I walked to Kharax[188] with Papa, the Aunt,

Mordvinov, Anya and Drenteln. It was hot: 18 degrees in the evening. Returned

to the beach in a motor and went swimming, which was delightful. Smirnov,

---

[188] Kharax was an English style palace in the Crimea, home to H.I.H. Grand Duke Georgi Mikhailovich, named after the largest Roman military settlement excavated in the Crimea. It was adjacent to the Palace of Ai-Todor.

Kublitzky, Kozhevnikov and Shepotiev were there. In the afternoon went to Ai-Danil, ate grapes, which were not yet ripe. Had tea and dinner on the balcony. Saw N.P. through the fieldglass, but wanted to see S. so much. Mama was hot all day long. Aleksei's right arm hurts a little. Played cards in the evening.

Saturday. 17 August. After 9 o'cl. we four walked in the vineyards with Papa and Aunt, then down to the beach and swam. Stayed in the water for a long time – the water is warm, and [there were] waves. At 11 1/2 went to the yacht. Papa reviewed the crew. Moleben was held on after-deck. Refreshments were [served] downstairs by the engine hatch. Breakfast was in the saloon. Stayed at the table until 2 o'cl. 45 min. I sat with Papa and N.P., and stared at my S. the whole time. I am now feeling so good because of that. Papa talked to the senior officers. We were going to leave, but then stayed for some reason and started dancing in the green dining room. First they played mazurka on the deck, then Shepotiev played the piano. It was such fun. I danced with my beloved S. a lot. We left at about 4 o'cl. Had tea with Mama on the balcony. Such a shame that she could not be there. She is still not feeling well and does not sleep well. It is 11 o'cl. 20 min. now and 19 degrees. Quiet, clear night. Went to vsenoshnaya. Dinner was downstairs. The officers who fought in the Kulm battle were there. The yacht was bright with illuminations. In the evening sat with Mama.

Sunday. 18 August. Obednya was held at 11 o'cl. After that – a big breakfast as usual. N.P. was there. In the afternoon we 4, Papa and Aunt went to Eriklik, the farm, and then walked to the beach where we swam for a long time. Did not see S., such a shame. Had tea on the balcony downstairs, had dinner upstairs. In the evening Papa read "Le Colin de la Reine" aloud. Mama's temperature was 37.6, yesterday it was 37.5. Her heart is not enlarged, but she is not feeling well all the time. [...]. Her feet ache and are swollen. May the Lord save her. N.P. sat with her for a while in the afternoon. So happy. 19 degrees.

Monday. 19 August. Severe thunderstorm at night and in the morning [it] rained. S. finally had breakfast, as well as Nevyarovsky, Batushka and Babitzyn. Before the walk, sat with S. on Anya's balcony for ¼ hour. So happy to see him. Walked in Oreanda and swam in the sea – big waves and lots of fun. Had tea downstairs on the balcony, dinner – upstairs. Mama's heart was 2 all day, temperature 37.4, pulse 88. Played cards with the Aunt. Papa read. It is cooler – 17 degrees. Clear, stars, summer lightning.

Tuesday. 20 August. The Shirvansky regiment squadron arrived. [We] walked in the vineyards and swam. Saw boating exercises from very far away. How I want to see S. Zlebov, Kozhevnikov, Shepotiev and Rodionov had breakfast. In the afternoon [we] hiked up the Ai-Petri mountain and [walked] through Yarikin's farm. Anya and I rode in the second motor. Returned through Uganez – 7 eagles were flying. It is chilly in the mountains. Daria Gesse[189] arrived at 6 o'cl. 15 min., and we sat with her until 7 o'cl. Summer lightning. Had dinner on the balcony.

---

[189] Daria Petrovna Gesse was the daughter of palace commandant and a friend of Olga's.

Mama's temperature is 37.4, [she is] pale and tired. Aleksei had his first mud bath in the sun. I also put some on my knees. 19 degrees, stars.

Olga on a balcony

Wednesday. 21 August. Walked to the vineyards and swam without swimsuits. Before breakfast Papa reviewed the 1st squadron of his Shirvansky regiment which arrived from Persia yesterday morning. Through a fieldglass sw S. get into a barge. N.P., Smirnov, Butakov and Kublitzky had breakfast. 24 degrees in the shade. A little chillier in the afternoon. There was a thunderstorm in town – we saw the lightning and heard the thunder. Walked to the farm and back. We four drank the milk, buttermilk and boiled varenetz[190] with Papa, the Aunt, Komarov, Drenteln and Mordvinov. Saw the children, the farmer and a 2-year-old bull that weighs 832 kg. Had tea on the balcony. Anya and N.P. took Mama down to the beach in a wheelchair. They came back in a motor. I am so happy that she had some amusement thank God, and she seems to feel better. Had dinner upstairs as usual. Everyone played cards. Mama was lying down. Papa read in French. Walked along the trail with Anya. 17 ½ degrees.

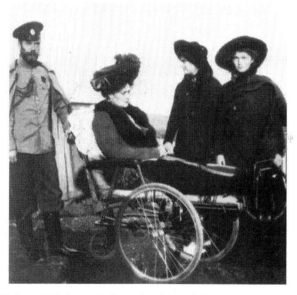

Olga and Tatiana with their parents. Alexandra often needed a wheelchair due to her health problems.

---

[190] Fermented milk, something like yogurt.

Thursday. 22 August. Walked in the vineyard. Papa and I swam. The others have either a runny nose or Bekker. Clear warm water. Saw N.P. and S. through the fieldglass. Rodionov, Batushka, Stolitza and S. had breakfast. Awfully happy to see him, [I] missed him so much. In the afternoon Papa went to Krasny Kamen[191]. We four walked with Anya, Rodionov and S. It was very nice. Sat on the well under the balcony with my S. until 3 ½. The others sat on a bench. Then went to see Mama on the balcony. Aleksei was there too. Accompanied them to Anya's [room], then they read. Had tea and dinner with Papa, Mama, the Aunt. In the evening Papa read. 18 degrees, summer lightning far away at sea. In the afternoon there was a thunderstorm in the mountains. [It was] sunny here.

Olga and Tatiana in a carriage with their little brother Aleksei.

---

[191] Literally "The Red Rock"

Friday. 23 August. We two went to the beach and at 10 1/2 Papa and I went swimming. Babitzyn, Nevyarovsky, Shepotiev and Kozhevnikov had breakfast. In the morning [I] saw S. through the fieldglass. Stayed home in the afternoon. Sat on the balcony and in the garden, worked, painted. Mama was lying down close by. Talked to N.P. on the telephone and looked through the fieldglass. Papa went to Uchansu[192]. After tea we four and Aunt went to [see] Count and Countess Apraksin, played with the children. Rode along the waterfront. In the evening Papa read to us. Played cards with Mama. M's temperature is 38.1, runny nose and ear ache. Summer lightning far away at sea. 17 degrees. Walked in the garden with Anya.

Olga with her siblings, mother and Aunt

---

[192] Waterfalls just outside of Yalta.

Saturday. 24 August. We two and Aunt went shopping in Yalta. It was fun to walk along the waterfront, [we] saw a lot of acquaintances. Saw AKSHV in a [horse drawn] cab. Kublitzky, Smirnov, N.P. and Butakov, who also came to play tennis, had breakfast. It rained earlier, hence everything was wet. Played 3 sets with N.P. against Papa and T – won 1 of them. Then played 1 more set with the beloved S. against Papa and Anya and lost – no matter. Things are still the same, as my S. says. Sunny, warm, nice. Had tea with them and Mama on the downstairs balcony. Marie is lying down but she feels better. Went to vsenoshnaya. Had dinner with the imperial suite. In the evening Papa read. Played cards, Mama did too. 16 1/2 degrees.

Sunday. 25 August. [I] have Bekker, which is why I stayed in the chapel with Aleksei during obednya. Big breakfast. In the afternoon everyone went to Massandra[193], but I remained with Mama on the balcony and read. Then sat with Marie. Had tea and dinner with Papa, Mama and the Aunt. Around 6 o'cl. we two went to [illeg.] and sat with Count and Countess Grabbe and Countess Trubetskaya. There was torrential rain and thunderstorm. Beautiful starry sky in the evening, very bright summer lightning in the sea. 14 degrees and windy. Mama's heart is No.1. Did not see my S. today.

---

[193] The Massandra Palace had been built in the French chateau style by Count Vorontsov-Dashkov, but was acquired by Emperor Alexander III in 1889, who hired architect Maximilian Messmacher. The palace was finished in 1900. Prince Lev Galitzin began the Massandra Winery in 1894, and the region was known for its delicious wines.

Monday. 26 August. Stayed in bed for a long time. S., Zlebov, Batushka and Stolitza had breakfast. Then [we] went to the Aunt's with S. and Zlebov and stayed with her for a while. She took pictures of us. It was so nice. In the afternoon [I] stayed home, and was happy about it. Papa, Aunt and A went to Simeiz to [see] Maltzev. I read on the balcony. Then N.P. arrived. Sat with M who is in bed, Mama too. Had tea in the sitting room. At 6 ½ we two went to Yalta with Anya. Walked along the waterfront, stopped by an apothecary and a shop, where we bought a scarf for Mama. Then went to the yacht in a horse-drawn cab. The crew walked along the pier, [I] saw everyone, but did not see anybody in town. It was lots of fun. On the way back ran into AKSHV in the vineyard. Had dinner inside since it's too chilly – 13 degrees and windy. In the evening played cards. Papa read. Mama's heart No. 2.

Olga and Tatiana

Tuesday. 27 August. We three went to Yalta with the Aunt. [We] shopped and walked along the waterfront. Did not see too many acquaintances. Saw S. through the fieldglass, then [saw] the boating exercises, then N.P., Rodionov, Smirnov, Kozhevnikov and Nevyarovsky had breakfast. M's temperature is normal, but she is still in bed. In the afternoon went to Krasny Kamen, but did not do any sightseeing – [it was] cloudy everywhere, damp, hailing and very cold. Had tea and dinner inside. In the afternoon Mama was outside in the garden. [Played] cards in the evening. Papa read.

Wednesday. 28 August. Walked. Everybody went swimming, but I did not –

waves and cold. N.P., Zlebov, Kublitzky and Shepotiev had breakfast. Went to

[see] Madame Zizi, who is in bed. Played tennis in the afternoon. Played 1 set

with Anya against Papa and T and lost. Then played one set with T against Anya

and A and finally 3 sets with my S. against T and Rodionov, but won only 1.

Mama sat there with N.P. Had tea in front of the house. Damp and cold. M is still

in bed. Had dinner in the yacht saloon. [I] sat with Papa and N.P. Left the table at

10 o'cl. Stefanesko played a dulcimer. Remarkably cozy. Stood on the deck with

S. Suddenly everyone started dancing on starboard quarter-deck. It was such

fun. Then [we] went on the cape, rode all around it in a wagon. When we

returned, we resumed dancing – I danced a lot with the dearest S. At 12 o'cl.

went downstairs and sat cozily by the engine hatch and listened to Stefanesko

until 1 o'cl. in the morning. The Black Sea Fleet String Orchestra was playing on

the deck. When we returned, Mama was in bed. May the Lord keep her.

"Suddenly everyone started dancing on starboard quarter-deck."

Thursday. 29 August. [I] was sitting and lying down on the rocks while the others swam. Rodionov, Butakov, Stolitza and Batushka had breakfast. I feel so awfully lonesome today without S. Saw him briefly through the fieldglass on the barge. In the afternoon we 3 (Marie is still in bed) walked to Kharax with Papa and the

Aunt. There we had a tour of the house and garden and tea with Aunt Minnie[194] and Uncle Georgi. Aunt Ksenia was also there. During obednya and vsenoshnaya [I] stayed in the chapel. Mama has a headache, she is very tired and [her] heart bothers her. N.P. and Anya took her to the beach in the afternoon, which is why she is tired. [Played] cards after dinner. Papa finished his French book and started to read Teffi.

"Saw him briefly through the fieldglass..."

---

[194] Princess Maria of Greece and Denmark , daughter of King George I of Greece and Grand Duchess Olga Konstantinovna.

Friday. 30 August. Walked in the vineyard and to the beach, went swimming. 17 degrees. We all almost drowned. So chilly, it almost pulled us away from the rope. Kublitzky, Smirnov, Nevyarovsky and Kozhevnikov had breakfast. Played tennis in the afternoon. Played 2 sets with Papa against Rodionov and T – won 1. Then played 3 more sets with S. against Papa and AKSHV, and won the last one. Heard the Cossacks from far away, etc. Today is AKSHV's name day. Had tea in front of the house. N.P., the commander and Rodionov were also there. Had tea in the garden in front of the house. Mama and Marie were also there. At 6 o'cl. we three went to Yalta with the Aunt. Walked along the waterfront and stopped by to [see] Zembinsky. Ran into N.P. and dear S. I was so happy about this and a lot of other things. All four of us had dinner with Papa, Mama, Aunt and Mordvinov. In the evening we two with the Aunt, N.P. and Rodionov rode to Oreanda in their motor along the highway, and to the end of the waterfront. Very nice moon, chilly, but my S. was not there. Had tea and went to bed. Mama is fine.

Saturday. 31 August. Swam with Aunt for the last time. Only 13 degrees, took one dip in the water. Left at 10 1/2. We two [rode] in 2 motors with Drenteln and Mordvinov. AKSHV came to bid farewell to the Aunt, [I] greeted them. The turns were ghastly. Arrived at Bakhchisarai[195] at 2 1/2, had breakfast there in the house, walked in the garden and the cemetery. Went to the monastery on a cliff, very beautiful. Then walked uphill to old city of Gufut-Kale. Only two old men live

---

[195] City in central Crimea

there. Had tea in the garden under a chestnut tree. Left a little after 6 o'cl. Aunt

Olga, the Princess and Mordvinov stayed and waited for the train. It is so sad that

she is leaving. Returned at 9 o'cl. with Drenteln and Stolitza. Foggy and cold on

Ai-Petri[196]. The moon. Mama's heart bothers her, she is tired. Saw my S. through

the fieldglass, N.P. too.

~

---

[196] Peak in the Crimean mountains

September

Sunday. 1 September. Went to obednya. After that – a big breakfast. 18 degrees and sunny. Tennis in the afternoon. Played 2 sets with Butakov against S. and T, and lost both. Papa played with Rodionov. Mama also came. Played 2 games with S. against Anya and Butakov. It started to rain and we stopped [playing]. Sat inside the little house and had tea there. After it stopped raining and we finished tea, we played tag. Papa and my S. chased us. [I] love him terribly. Did not do anything until dinner. In the evening we two drove to Ai-Danil[197] with Papa and Anya. Returned through the Lower Massandra. Sandra Petrovskaya was visiting Mama. Mama is tired and not feeling well. 15 degrees, raining.

Monday. 2 September. Went to Oreanda, but I stayed in the water less than a minute – too cold. 3 officers from the 9th Kazansky Dragoon regiment, Zlebov, S., Stolitza had breakfast. It rained and was wet when we started playing tennis. Played 2 sets with N.P. against S. and T and lost miserably. Then we switched, but lost again. N.P., Rodionov and Petrovsky were also there. Then played American tennis with S. and T, switched places. Had tea inside upstairs, since Mama's heart is not good, and she could not come down to the garden. I sat with S. So happy to see so much of him. Had dinner on the balcony. In the evening

---

[197] A beach area in Hurzuf, near Yalta

we 2 played cards with Mama. Her heart is enlarged. May the Lord save her. Papa read in his [room]. Full moon, bright, surf, chilly.

Tuesday. 3 September. Had religion and French lessons. Then [we] went to the beach with Papa and swam. 15 degrees in the water. Saw S. through the fieldglass. N.P., Ippolit, Batushka and Rodionov had breakfast. Played tennis in the afternoon. Played 2 sets with N.P. against S. and T. I started out badly without S., and that's why [we] kept losing. Lost 1 set with Anya against Papa and T, and lost again with N.P. against Rodionov and T. Mama was there too. Petrovsky [too]. Had tea in the garden. I sat with S. It was nice but sad. At 6 o'cl., read. Had dinner on the balcony. After that rode to Ai-Todor[198] in a motor with Papa, T and Anya. [Someone] was shooting rockets across the road. Drove to the yacht and then turned around to go back. S. was on watch duty. Mama's temperature is 37.3. Chilly, quiet, nice. The moon.

Wednesday. 4 September. Went to Oreanda with Papa and T, then swam. 17 degrees. Butakov and Kozhevnikov had breakfast (they also played tennis), Nevyarovsky and Smirnov. 20 degrees in the shade. Countess Trubetskaya also came over. Won 1 set with T. against Papa and A. I lost 2 single sets to Anya 4-6. N.P. and Rodionov were also there, but S. is on watch duty since 4 o'cl, and I feel lonesome without him. Mama was there too. Had tea in the garden. Her temperature keeps rising and [her] heart is enlarged. In the morning [her]

---

[198] Town on a cape near Yalta

temperature was 37.4, in the evening the heart was No.2 and she does not feel well. 17 degrees in the evening. We two rode in motors with Papa and Anya [...]

Author's note: the rest of this entry was crossed out, probably by Olga herself.

Thursday. 5 September. Had lessons. At 11 o'cl. we two went swimming with Papa. Water temperature is 17 1/2 degrees. N.P., Zlebov (they also played tennis), Kublitzky and Stolitza, also a few old Cavalry Guard soldiers had breakfast. Today is their regimental holiday. Played 1 set with Anya against Papa and T, and lost. Then [played] with M [and] won against Zlebov and A. Mama came too, and sat in the shade (20 degrees) with N.P. Finally, played a single game with S. He got 6, I got 3. [I was] so happy to see him. Had not seen him for 1 day. Had tea in the garden, sat with him. In the morning the French yacht "The Jeanne Blanche", arrived from Constantinople. After dinner we 2 went to Massandra with Papa and Anya, watched the moon and saw a camel. Mama still does not feel well. 17 degrees.

"We 2"

Friday. 6 September. Walked in the vineyards with T and Papa, and then went swimming. 18 degrees, nice, ripples on the water. 4 French sailors from the yacht "The Jeanne Blanche" had breakfast, also Rodionov, Shepotiev, Ippolit and Babitzyn. [We] played 2 sets of tennis: one with Anya against Papa and T, which we lost, and one more with Butakov against Anya and T, which we won. N.P. and Nevyarovsky. My S. was there too. [I] sat with him at tea and tennis. Mama also came, she reclined under the bushes. Had dinner on the balcony with Papa, Mama, Aunt Minnie and Uncle Georgi. Spent the entire evening together there.

Today is a month since Count Nirod's death. May the Lord save us. 16 degrees. The moon is getting smaller.

Saturday. 7 September. We two had lessons until 11 o'cl. Then went to the beach to swim. Waves and very warm. 18 degrees, warmer than yesterday. The Jeanne Blanche left. S., Butakov, Batushka and Smirnov, also Count L. Golitsyn, who was yelling and saying funny things, had breakfast. Played tennis. S., N.P. and Rodionov. Played 2 sets with S. against N.P. and N.T., and won both. Sat on a bench. Then played one more set with Papa against S. and Anya, and won: 6-8. 20 degrees in the shade. Mama was there. Had tea in the garden. Sat with S. He is so good and sweet. Went to vsenoshnaya and had dinner downstairs. In the evening we 2 sat with Mama and Anya on the balcony. Papa read Irakli Lyapunov.

Sunday. 8 September. Went to obednya and had a big breakfast. AKSHV was there, too. I talked to him – such a darling. In the afternoon went to Krasny Kamen. It was nice and sunny, warm, and S. was there. N.P. and Rodionov also came. Walked around and returned at about 6 o'cl. We three rode in a motor. M stayed with Mama. Had dinner on the balcony. Mama does not feel well. Pulse is 96, the heart is beating [too fast]. In the morning [her] temperature was 37.2, I think. Papa read. May the Lord save us.

Monday. 9 September. We two went to Oreanda with Papa and then went swimming. 18 1/2 degrees, wonderful. Saw S. through the fieldglass. A delegation from Apsheronsky regiment had breakfast, also Stolitza, Zlebov, Nevyarovskiy and Kozhevnikov. Tennis in the afternoon. Won 2 sets with Rodionov against Papa and N.P., and 1 set with Anya against S. and M. Mama and Stolitza also came. Had tea in the garden. 20 degrees in the shade. We four had dinner with Papa in the saloon. It was very nice. Paladino played. Then [we] danced on the deck. S. filled in for Stolitza for a while while he had dinner. Then [we] went down to the green parlor, played various games and romped crazily. First [we] played something like riddles – split up into 2 teams, then played dobchinsky-bobchinsky, forfeitures, turkey, threw a scarf around [and] hid in dark cabins and laughed a lot. At the end [we] played the charades. I was on S.'s team every time and was awfully happy. We had the word "sheep". Kublitzky, Shepotiev, Zlebov and Babitzyn were with us. T had "puffin". Rodionov, Stolitza, Ippolit and Butakov. [We] laughed so hard, [it was] incredibly wonderful. Papa played kosti. [We] left at 11 1/2. Mama was already in bed.

Tuesday. 10 September. Had lessons, after that went swimming with A and Papa. 18 1/2 degrees. S., Kublitzky, Ippolit and Babitzev had breakfast. Tennis in the afternoon. Played 4 sets with Rodionov: 2 against Papa and Butakov, and won 1. 2 – against Papa and Anya, and won both. It was fun, but [I felt] empty and sad without my beloved S. N.P. also was there, [he] sat with Mama. Had tea in the garden – warm. Had dinner on the balcony. Warm. Evening lightning far away. Papa read, we worked. Mama's heart aches and she does not feel well. Spoke on the telephone with Papa [sic?].

Wednesday. 11 September. Went to the beach swimming with Papa. 18 degrees. Then a thunderstorm came, heavy rain. A little after 11 o'cl. Papa went to Alushta[199] in a motorboat. From there he drove to the Kosmodemiansky monastery in a motor for hunting and overnight stay. Had breakfast and dinner with Mama upstairs. In the afternoon [we] organized things for the bazaar in the spare room. Mama came too. N.P., Rodionov, Shepotiev, Anya, Trina, Sonia, Olga Yevg[enievna], Drenteln and Petrovsky were there too. Then [we] had tea all together. Again after 9 o'cl. The ladies, S. (I was very worried that I would not see him today), Kublitzky, Stolitza and Shepotiev also came. My S., how I love him. Heavy rain, 13 degrees. Mama's heart is No.3, but despite that she still helped.

Thursday. 12 September. Had lessons and did not do anything. Papa returned in a motor for breakfast. Very chilly out in the sea. Butakov, Shepotiev, Rodionov and Batushka came for breakfast. Saw my S. through the fieldglass: during the boating exercises and at watch duty on the left front ramp. Besides that did not see him all day and I feel sad. In the afternoon we four and Papa walked along Mama's carriage. Went to Oreanda by the sea, watched the surf. Overcast – no sun, no my S. On the way back it started to rain heavily. Had tea and dinner with Papa and Mama. Rain – chilly. After 7 o'cl. read with M. Gilliard as usual.

---

[199] City on the Southern cost of the Crimea

Mama's heart was not enlarged all day – finally. In the evening [we] sat together working for the bazaar. Mama embroidered and dyed a lot. Anya came over after 10 o'cl. Sat and did not do anything. Went to bed at about 11. May the Lord save everyone. 13 degrees.

Petrovsky. Friday. Livadia. 13 September, 1913. At first I sat at home because of the rain, then walked around the vineyards with Papa. N.P., S., Kozhevnikov, Zlebov had breakfast. In the afternoon Papa walked with three of the consolidated troops but we stayed home, which I don't regret. I had such a good time with S. and N.P. We sat at Mama's. S. pasted the last of things for the bazaar. I sat nearby and felt so happy to see him. I did not see him all day yesterday and really missed him. After that we 4 played cards in the other room with him and Anya. Then we played the grand piano for him. When Papa returned, we had tea. It poured all day. Mama has a headache. Went to Vsenoshnaya. In the evening Papa read Prokopi Lyapunov. We worked. 12 degrees.

Olga and Tatiana with "Mama" in Livadia

Saturday. 14 September. Went to obednya and vsenoshnaya. Stolitza,

Nevyarovsky, Ippolit and Grandmama had breakfast. Both of them played tennis.

Played 2 sets against T. and Anya. We won 1 set and lost 1 set with Anya

against Papa and T. Papa played a single against Rodionov. Mama came too.

She reclined under the bushes. It started to rain and we had tea in the cabin

earlier than usual. Ran into my S. riding in a motor with the Kleinmichels. I am lonesome when he is not around. Had dinner with the suite and after that played [cards?]. [It was] so nice. Reminisced about Yalta.

Sunday. 15 September. Went to obednya. Mama was in the chapel. After that had a big breakfast, talked to the guards and Svodny troops. 16 degrees. Sunny in the morning, overcast in the afternoon. Played tennis. I played 2 sets with S. against N.P. and T., won both. Then sat with S. on a bench in Grinogoreiskoe, and finally played a single. Mama was sitting with Stolitza. Papa played with Rodionov. Tea was served outside. My S. is not feeling well, the poor darling. May the Lord keep him. In the evening Papa read 2 stories by Averchenko to us. Very funny. We smoked and worked. Mama too. Aleksei was so cute with Shotol. M and A went to Kharaks.

Kosmodemyansky. Monday. 16 September. Studied. It was cool out in the sea. At 11.38 we two went in motors to Kosmodemyansky with Papa and Drenteln. Saw S. on the seafront. I felt awfully happy. We [had to] stop on the way because T wasn't [feeling] well. After 12 o'cl. we passed by Alushta. Arrived at 2 o'cl. 15 min., ate, and then Papa went hunting. He returned at 7 o'cl. Picked dogwood berries with Drenteln and Shura. Made cookies and jam on the porch. It's warm in the sun, 16 degrees. It is so beautiful here. Alma[200] is rumbling down there. Walked after tea. Before dinner and before evening we 2 played kosti with Papa and Drenteln. Mama talked on the telephone. We 2 sleep in the same room with Shura. Cold. Walked until it got dark. Stars. Clear.

---

[200] A river

Olga and her family in Livadia

Tuesday. 17 September. Livadia. Papa went hunting at 3 o'clock. Killed a good deer. We got up at 6 o'cl. and went to obednya at 7 o'cl. Papa returned at 9 o'cl., we ate and sat in front of the house until 12 o'cl. He sat with Drenteln on a bench, and we sat with Shura. At first we ran around with a net chasing each other, then [we] read. [We] left at 1 o'clock. Stopped to walk in the same spot. Got home at 3 1/2. Saw my S. on the deck in Yalta. N.P. and Anya rode in motors. Had tea and dinner with Papa and Mama. She is fine, thank God. I am happy to be here

232

closer to her and S. Worked in the evening. The long motor rides really made me [feel] silly.

Wednesday. 18 September. Had lessons. Aunt Militza[201], Uncle Petusha, Marina, Elena, Rodionov, Smirnov, Butakov and Kublizsky had breakfast. Tennis in the afternoon. Played two sets with T against N.P. and lost. Also played 2 singles against N.P. and lost. Papa played with Rodionov. Petrovsky was also there. My S. is not here, and I feel lonesome. Had tea upstairs at home because Mama stayed [home]. Her heart is not enlarged. Sat at Isa Buxhoeveden's until dinner. In the evening Papa read Averchenko to us and we worked. Strong wind.

---

[201] H.I.H. Grand Duchess Militza Nikolaevna, wife of Grand Duke Peter Nikolaevich ("Uncle Petusha"), son of Grand Duke Nikolai Nikolaevich ("Nikolasha").

"Sat at Isa Buxhoeveden's until dinner." Olga and Tatiana with Sophie Buxhoeveden (left).

Thursday. 19 September. Walked to church via the horizontal path with Papa and smoked on a bench in Livadia. Stolitza, Shepotiev, Kozhevnikov and Batushka, as well as the Georgian regiment delegation, had breakfast. Tennis in the afternoon. Played 4 sets against Rodionov and T., 2 sets with N.P., we lost. Also played 2 sets with Papa. We lost one, and they lost one. Butakov was there too, as well as Mama. Aleksei's right arm hurts. Did not see S., and I feel lonesome. Papa read Teffi, Mama and we worked.

Friday. 20 September. Studied. At 10 o'clock Papa left for Kosmodemyansk. Had breakfast and tea with Mama. Had dinner with her and Shura. Walked along Mama's carriage in the afternoon. N.P. and Anya also came. At 4 o'clock we 4 went to the Festivities Hall with Olga Yevgenievna to lay things out for the bazaar. My S. and dear friends helped. He still is not feeling well, has a cough. I am awfully happy to see him. I was lonesome for 2 days without him. Returned at 6 1/2, after making all the arrangements. 10 degrees in the evening. We signed various Tatar towels until 10 1/2. Mama did too. Talked to Papa on the telephone.

"Walked along Mama's carriage..."

Saturday. 21 September. Went horseback riding. Rode Bystry there and Mars back. Awfully nice. Papa returned at about 12 o'cl. and we all had breakfast with Mama. Played tennis in the afternoon. Played one set with Papa against Anya and N.P. Then sat with Mama. N.P. and Zlebov were also there. Bekker arrived. Butakov also. It's so dreadful without my S., terrible. Had tea in the garden. Had dinner with everyone downstairs. Marked merchandise until 11 o'cl. Chilly. Papa shot a deer.

Sunday. 22 September. [I] stayed in bed until breakfast. Papa and M went to Alupka for consecration of some church. When they returned we all had breakfast with Papa and Mama. At 2 o'clock we five went to the bazaar in Yalta with Mama. AKSHV was the first one to buy from me. N.P. and other officers came. Ladies-in-waiting Olga and Tasha Kleinmichel, Marusia and Vera Trepova, as well as Daria Gesse helped [us]. It was very nice but exhausting. My head feels empty and aches. Mama left for the yacht at 4 o'clock. We left at 6. I sat on the deck until dinner, and finally my S. came. He has a cold and [is] coughing. So tiresome. At 9 o'clock we 4 went down to the bazaar again. S. went too. The Yerivansky regiment shopped: Otar M., Ravtopulo, Prince Ernestov and Prince Shervanidze. Returned at 11 o'cl. Saw AKSHV again. Walked. The day went well, thank God. I just want S. to get better.

"...We[...] went to the bazaar in Yalta..." Olga and her sisters working at the charity bazaar booth.

Monday. 23 September. [I] was lying in bed for a while. S., Zlebov, Nevyarovsky and Babintzev had breakfast. Went to the bazaar from 2 to 6 o'clock and 9 to 11 o'clock. There were masses of people. AKSHV was there, [I] saw him a lot. N.P. came in the afternoon, helped to sell things. My S. was also here, but he was at the refreshments bar upstairs with the Ivanenkos, so I only saw him from far away. Had dinner with Papa. Mama was on the balcony. She is very tired and did not go to the bazaar. In the morning it was 21 degrees in the shade and 32 degrees in the sun. 15 degrees at night. Grigori Yefimovich had tea with Papa, Mama and Anya.

Tuesday. 24 September. Stayed in bed for a while. Studied a French lesson at 11 o'cl. Rodionov, Batushka, Kublitzky and Smirnov had breakfast. Went to the bazaar at 2 o'clock and returned at 4 o'clock. Saw AKSHV and my S. from far away. They were upstairs with the Ivanenkos. After we returned [we] went to play tennis. I sat with Mama and N.P. Papa played with Rodionov, etc. Had tea in the garden. Very warm, 21 degrees in the shade in the afternoon. 7 degrees at night. Had dinner on the balcony. In the evening we 4 and Papa went to Narodny Dom for a concert. Plevitzkaya, Stefanesko, Raisova, gypsy romance songs, 4 singers and a quartet – 3 Preobrazhensky regiment members and a harp player E. L. Grishinskaya, wife of a commander from the grenadier regiment, very nice. Returned at 11 1/2. My S. was not there, he is on watch duty.

Aerial shot of the Yalta charity bazaar

239

Wednesday. 25 September. Had lessons. Babitzyn, Shepotiev, Ippolit and Kozhevnikov had breakfast. Tennis in the afternoon. Before that Sandra Petrovna visited Mama. I played 2 sets with Papa against N.P. and T., and we won. Then played with M. and A. Mama was there too. Had tea in the garden. It [was] cloudy in the mountains. Had dinner on the balcony and at 9 o'cl. went to the Durov circus. It was lots of fun. On the way there [we] saw Grigori Yefimovich. The Cossacks, the sailors, the soldiers and the entire Livadia were there. My beloved S. too. So happy to see him and N.P. Returned at 11 1/2. Mama has a headache. Very tired. 14 degrees.

The imperial family in Livadia

Thursday. 26 September. In the morning N.P., Ira and I went shopping in Yalta. Watched the boat maneuvers. S. came in first on the second boat in the first race. N.P., Smolitza, Butakov and Nevyarovsky had breakfast. Tennis in the afternoon. Won 2 sets with Anya against N.P. and T. Also played 2 sets with S. against Papa and Anya, and won one set. Then just sat with S., so sweet and kind. Had tea in the garden. Damp. Mama was there too. 12 degrees in the evening. Had dinner with Papa, Mama, Aunt Ksenia, Uncle Sandro and Irina. My S. keeps coughing, he has a bad cold.

Friday. 27 September. Zlebov, Batushka and Kublitzky had breakfast, but my S. got sick at the last minute and did not come. Did not see him all day and [I] miss him. Played three sets with Papa against Rodionov and T. and won two sets. One was a tie, another – 9:7. Then played 2 singles with T and won. Mama was there too. She has been feeling nauseous all day and has a stomach ache. Had tea in the garden. Had dinner on the balcony. In the evening we 2 rode in a motor with Papa and Anya. Saw Grigori Yefimovich and N.P. in Yalta. Drove through the Lower Massandra – moon, nice – 13 degrees.

Saturday. 28 September. Rode horses to Ai-Nikola, the farm and Livadia community. Ran into AKSHV who was walking. Such a darling. N.P., Smirnov, Shepotiev and the Erivansky regiment officers had breakfast. In the afternoon pasted in albums with Papa, Mama and Anya. S., N.P. and Rodionov arrived at about 4 o'clock. S. pasted photos for me. At about 4 1/2 [we] left for Ai-Todor. I

241

really did not want to leave my S. Went to Vsenoshnaya and had dinner with everyone downstairs. In the evening sat at Mama's, smoked and worked. Mama has a backache. She is nauseous and does not feel well. 10 degrees.

Sunday. 29 September. Went to obednya. Played tennis in the afternoon. Won 1 set with Papa against Anya and T, then won 2 sets with him against T and Rodionov. Then sat with Babitzyn and [was] freezing. Mama was with N.P. My dear S. was not there, and I was angry and lonesome. Had tea at home. Had dinner with Papa, Mama, K. and Uncle Mitya. Sat all together in the evening. 5 1/2 degrees.

Olga

Monday. 30 September. At 10 in the morning we two went to Yalta with Papa to an exhibition of the Crimean produce in Town Park. Stolitza, Ippolit, Kozhevnikov and Babitzyn had breakfast. [It is] terribly cold. Tennis in the afternoon. Played 3 sets with Papa against T and Rodionov, and won 2. Then stayed with Mama and N.P. I feel so sad that I have not seen S. for two days now. Came back in a motor and had tea in Mama's purple lounge. Went to vsenoshnaya. Had dinner with Papa and Mama in the dining room. It is windy [and it] sounds like someone is knocking on the door. Spoke on the telephone with AKSHV for the first time and was very happy. Papa asked if Zborovsky returned from Yevpatoria. Such a darling.

~

October

Tuesday. 1 October. Went to obednya. Mama also came but stayed in the chapel. Rodionov, Kublitzky, Zlebov, and Nevyarovsky had breakfast. Cold and very windy. Played tennis. Played 2 sets with Anya against N.P. and T., a tie. Then played "bumble" with Ippolit. Papa played with Anya, T. and Rodionov. Mama was with N.P. After the game [we] went down to the beach to look at the surf. S. is in Kosmodemyansk, so what. However, it is awfully lonesome without him. [I] want to see him, as well as dear AKSHV. Had tea in Mama's purple sitting room. After dinner we 2 walked in Papa's jacket. 5 degrees.

Wednesday. 2 October. Had lessons. At 11 in the morning we 2 and Ira went shopping in Yalta. Ippolit, Butakov, Batushka and Shepotiev had breakfast. Tennis in the afternoon. Won 1 set with Papa against Rodionov and T., and lost 2 sets. Very cold. Then played with M. against A. and Kublitsky. Had tea in Mama's purple sitting room. N.P. sat with Mama. I am now accustomed to not seeing S. for so long, and feel his absences less, even though I do miss him a lot. Marusia and Vera Trepova visited in the evening at 7. Worked in the evening. Mama's heart is No.1. 6 degrees.

Olga, Anastasia and Maria with their mother and N.P. Sablin

Thursday. 3 October. We 2 and Olga Yevgenievna finally rode horses with

AKSHV and Zborovsky. Rode through Livadia, "mon jardin", a farm and Eriklyk.

[We] sat in a gazebo there for a while, and I really enjoyed it. SH was sweet as

usual. He was [wearing] my favorite dark jacket and [riding] a red horse named

Boy, but it was not his. [We] rode down a trail. I enjoyed it profoundly. Sunny,

clear. At 9 o'clock Papa and others drove through Krasny Kamni, then walked to

Kosmodemyansk. Returned at about 6 in the evening. Played tennis. 2 sets with

M. against T. and A., lost. Then won a single against Anya. Then played 2 sets with N.P. against T. and Rodionov. Lost one set with Anya against them. Mama was there. Cold. 8 degrees at night. Worked with Mama. Papa read. Anya came after 10. French reading at 7, as usual. Still don't see my S., but miss him less.

Friday. 4 October. Had lessons until 11. At 11 ½ we five went to the Escort barracks with Papa and, thank God, Mama. The molebna and parade were held there in honor of the holiday. It was very nice. After breakfast [I] talked with the officers in the courtyard. Spoke to dear AKSHV, [and] was very happy. Tennis in the afternoon. Played 2 sets with Papa against Rodionov and T., a tie. Then we watched the saluting navy squadron and finally [I] saw S., first in a motor, and then with the platoon. My S. also saw me. Had tea at home with Butakov. N.P. left earlier. Nastenka Hendrikova came over. Went to vsenoshnaya and moleben. Not surprisingly Mama is very tired: after the parade and all the talking after breakfast. 5 1/2 degrees.

Saturday. 5 October. At 11 there was a molebna and parade of the escort troops stationed here, AKSHV with the Svodny regiment, a platoon from the yacht with my S., a squadron of the Lithuanian regiment, the Vilemsky platoon, a platoon of the 16th infantry regiment, a platoon of the Shirvansky regiment, a platoon of the Crimean regiment, the torpedo boat crew, and a platoon of the border patrol. After that – a massive breakfast. Papa awarded the ranks of warrant officers to the midshipmen. Tennis in the afternoon. Won 1 set with Anya against Papa and T., then lost 3 sets with Papa against T. and Rodionov. Won 2 other sets. N.P.

sat with Mama. Then played a single with A. Grigori Yefimovich came over at
6.15, and we sat all together. Went to Vsenoshnaya at the chapel. Aleksei wore a
new jacket. He received a Georgian regiment uniform. I am lonesome without my
S. In the evening we 4 and Papa drove to the yacht through Yalta. [We] watched
the illumination of the fleet, the city and the banners. 5 1/2 degrees. Mama is
tired because of the parade and the breakfast.

"We 4 and Papa"

Sunday. 6 October. Went to obednya. Big breakfast as usual. Tennis in the afternoon. Lost 2 sets with Papa against Rodionov and T. N.P. sat with Mama. After that had tea at home. Tasha and Olga Kleinmichel were here before dinner. So lonesome without S. 10 degrees in the evening. Finally, it was warm the entire day. The fleet left at midnight last night. Mama is tired.

Monday. 7 October. T. and I had lessons. I had French and religion until 11 1/2. S., Stolitza, Kozhevnikov and Smirnov. Tennis in the afternoon. Finally my S. and A. played 3 sets against T. and me. They won 1, and we won 2. Papa played with Rodionov, then again with Rodionov, S. and Anya. I sat with Mama. She has a severe headache, poor darling. Had tea at Mama's [I] sat with S. and was so happy. Overcast but warm. Sunny in the morning, windy in the evening. 10 degrees. Read in French and Russian. After dinner worked at Mama's […] N.P. wil be taking the harp player to Sevastopol and stopped by Papa's.

Tuesday. 8 October. Had a Russian language lesson at 11. Before that we 2 and Ira went to the beach to watch the high tide. Zlebov, Rodionov, Babitzyn and Nevyarovsky had breakfast. Played tennis. Played 1 set with A. against Papa and M. and then 3 more with Rodionov against Papa and N.P. We won 2 sets, and they won 1. Mama was lying down nearby. Did not see S., lonesome. Had tea at home since Uncle Sandro, Aunt Ksenia and Irina came over. Then – French reading. Mama went to Yalta to see Grigori Yefimovich. After that she went to a glass store and bought a vase for each of us. Darling. She is terribly tired. [...] She did well. In the evening [I] helped Anya paste in the album.

Wednesday. 9 October. Had a Russian and Religion lessons until 11 o'clock. At 11 ½ we 2 with Papa and Aleksei went to the Shirvansky regiment. There was a moleben and a parade for the 25-th anniversary of the Shirvansky regiment. Took group pictures. Then had breakfast with them at our [place]. Saw AKSHV from far away. Played tennis in the afternoon. 3 sets with Rodionov against Papa and Shaprinsky, won only 1 set. Then 2 more sets with Shurik[202]; lost against Shaprinsky and A. Lots of fun. I was glad that he was finally invited. Had tea together at Mama's. She has a headache, but is fine thank God. N.P. was there. We 2 and Papa went to Ai-Todor for dinner. After dinner we 2 and Irina played hide-and-seek in a dark room with my S., Rodionov and Felix. We played until 11 ½ o'cl. It was such fun. I was with my S. We looked for others together. N.P. was also there. Returned at about midnight. Mama was still up. Anya returned from Bakhchisarai, she took Grigori Yefimovich there. Thank God for today. A good day. 6 degrees in the evening.

---

[202] Most likely this again is Alexander Konstatinovich Shvedov, who was probably also "AKSHV" as well as "Sh."

"N.P. was also there." Olga and Tatiana with Sablin and some other officers

Thursday. 9 October [sic - should read 10 October]. Walked to Oreanda with Papa, then along the beach – to Livadia, and from there took a motor to the Russian lesson. The Crimean regiment officers had breakfast. Today is the anniversary of Mama's arrival in the Crimea 19 years ago[203], and 4 years ago she was appointed honorary chief of the regiment. Then she went downstairs. Papa bid farewell to the crew who were retiring from the yacht, and Mama presented them with watches and money. Tennis in the afternoon. 2 sets with

[203] Just prior to the death of Alexander III.

Anya against Papa and T., and one single [set] each as well as an American set without N.P., who sat with Mama. She is fine, thank God, no backache. At 9 in the evening [we] went to the circus. Very funny. I was especially happy that Shurik and my S. were there. Returned at 11 1/2. Starry sky, moon, 6 3/4 degrees. Mama and Anya had tea when we returned.

Friday. 11 October. We 2 had Russian lesson until 10 in the morning. Saw off the ship with the sailors who moved to the reserves. They waved their caps and yelled "hurrah" [when passed] by Livadia. We also waved, [it was] very sad. Papa left at 8 ½ in the morning to hike through Krasny Kamni to Ai-Petri and back, planned to return for tea. [We] had breakfast with Mama. She has a lot of pain in [her] lower back. Tennis in the afternoon. Played 2 sets with S. against T. and N.P. Then played with S. against T. and Anya. Then with Anya against S. and T., and, finally, with T. against S. and Anya. I played extremely badly and kept losing. Returned for tea with S., Anya and T. N.P. went to the Shirvansky regiment. Aleksei has a pain in his leg and did not go outside. Worked in the evening. Papa read Averchenko's stories. 8 degrees.

Saturday. 12 October. Had a French lesson at 11. Before that we 2 went to the beach with Nastenka and Ira, very warm. Count and Countess Vorontsov, N.P., S., Batushka and Kublitsky had breakfast. 27 degrees in the sun, 15 degrees in the shade and 11 degrees in the evening. Played tennis: 2 sets with Anya against Papa and T., then again with S. against them. Won and lost with T.

against S. and A. Mama sat with N.P. Aleksei was lying in the sun, [he] felt a bit better. S. is so cheerful and nice today. Had tea at home. I sat with him. Went to vsenoshnaya. Had dinner downstairs. In the evening Papa read Apukhtin.

Olga with her mother

Sunday. 13 October. Big breakfast after obednya. In the afternoon Papa went to Ai-Danil with some of the suite and then walked to Massandra. We 2 played tennis with Anya and Rodionov, all possible sets: singles, etc. Returned for tea. Papa did too. Mama stayed home with N.P. The sisters went to Kharaks. Aleksei is lying down in a chair downstairs. Did not see S. and it was sad. Sat at Nastenka's until dinner. She read, I worked. The English book Vixen. In the evening worked at Mama's. Papa read in his [room]. 7 degrees.

Monday. 14 October. Had lessons. After that we 2 walked with Nastenka. Butakov, Kozhevnikov, Stolitza and Ippolit had breakfast. Tennis in the afternoon. Played 2 sets with Papa against T. and Rodionov, won 1 set each. Mama sat with N.P., her back still aches. Had tea at home with them. After dinner went to wish Aleksei a good night as usual. He is better. At 9.15 in the evening we 2 went to a charity ball at Narodny Dom with Papa, Aunt Ksenia and Irina, benefit for the institution and temperance. Came back at about 11 at night. It was lots of fun. I danced 1 quadrille with Prince Trubetskoy[204]. He was also the conductor. The 2nd dance, which was the cotillion, I danced with Volodi Gantskau, the waltz – with N.P. and with dear Shurik, who was very jolly in his dark jacket. Saw my S. once – he passed in the quadrille. He seemed sad somehow, I don't know. There was a troika with ribbons. Shurik and another sailor [rode in it?]. When we returned [we] had tea with Mama.

[204] Prince Nikolai Sergeyevich Trubetskoy was a Russian linguist and historian at court.

Tuesday. 15 October. Walked through the vineyards and to the beach with Papa. Colonel Ofinovsky of my regiment, an officer of M.'s regiment, Rodionov, Shepotiev, Babitzyn and Nevyarovsky had breakfast. Papa went to Alupka to [visit] the children's sanatorium. [We] played tennis: 2 sets with N.P. against T. and Rodionov, then different singles, 3 sets altogether. Mama was there. Had tea as usual. Had dinner in Kharaks. Aunt Ksenia, Irina, Uncle Mitya also came over. Felix came over later. Played cards, animal names, almost until 12 o'cl. I feel lonesome without S. Mama has a severe headache. Clear, chilly. 6 degrees in Kharax at 9 1/2.

Wednesday. 16 October. Had lessons. At 11 o'cl, we 2 and Anya walked to the farm. At 8 1/2 Papa left for Krasny Kamen, etc. Returned for tea. Had breakfast with Mama. She still has a headache, although not as bad. She came to tennis and sat with N.P. First we 4 played 1 1/2 sets, then Anya and I played 2 sets against Rodionov and T. and lost both. Then Shurik and Zborovsky came. Won 1 set with A against Shurik and M. Then played 2 sets with M against them, a tie. Laughed a lot, it was such fun. Saw my S. through the fieldglass, very nice. Sat with Mama after dinner. Aleksei walked around a bit. 8 degrees.

Thursday. 17 October. We 2 rode horses to Ugansa. I rode Mars as usual, but he was not as full of energy as usual. Ran into Shurik on horseback. He was on duty, checking outposts in his blue uniform. Butakov, Kublitzky, Smirnov and Ippolit had breakfast. Tennis in the afternoon. Won 2 sets and lost 1 set with

Shurik against Butakov and A. 5:7 against N.P. and T. Papa played a single [set] with Zborovsky. Had tea with them at home. On the way back ran into the Kleinmichels in a motor. Sometimes I really miss S. After dinner sat with Mama and worked. She still has a headache, although not as bad. 10 degrees. It was the first day that I felt warm during tennis.

"Papa played a single [set] with Zborovsky." Sitting left to right: Viktor Erastovich Zborovsky, Tatiana, Anna Vyrubova, Olga and Nicholas II on a tennis court. Anastasia is standing behind them.

Friday. 18 October. Had lessons. At 11 in the morning we 2, Nastenka and Ira went shopping in Yalta. Batushka, Shepotiev, Rodionov and Kozhevnikov had breakfast. Tennis in the afternoon. Overcast, chilly. Won 1 set with A. against M.

and Shanpersky. Lost 2 sets with N.P. against Shanpersky and T, then played 1 set with Papa against T and Rodionov. Mama was there and after 6 in the evening [she] went to a chapel in Yalta. Zborovsky was there too. Had tea as usual. Shurik was not invited. Such a shame. S. left for Bakhchisarai and Simferopol, so [I] did not see him. After dinner sat with Mama. Papa read the report from torpedo boats. Windy. 8 degrees. Washed [our] hair.

Saturday. 19 October. Went to the beach with Nastenka and Ira, medium waves. The following had breakfast: N.P. (he was at tennis, too), Babitzyn (also), Zlebov and Ippolit. Played 1 set with Anya against Papa and T., and 1 set with Papa against Rodionov and T. It is boring because the Cossacks aren't here. S. returned around 2 o'clock, but I did not see him. So be it. Went to vsenoshnaya. After dinner looked at photographs with Papa and Mama. She is better, thank God. 8 degrees. New moon.

Sunday. 20 October. Went to obednya even though was not feeling well. Mama was in the chapel. Had breakfast upstairs. Aunt Ksenia and Lili, Uncle Mitya and Georgi, Irina, Nikita and T[illeg.] came over. At 2 o'cl. went to Grandpapa's house and the rooms where he passed away. There was a panikhida. After that we 4 went to Oreanda to the Mast Hill with Papa and Mama, then to the beach and then returned home, [illeg.] of course. Had tea and dinner together. Went to vsenoshnaya and at 9 ½ o'cl. confessed in the chapel. Did not see anyone, including S. Thank you, God.

Monday. 21 October. At 9 in the morning went to obednya and received communion. After that had tea all together. I sat on Mama's balcony and read. The sisters walked with Mama. Papa and Aleksei rode in a dvoika[205]. Had breakfast and dinner all together upstairs. Played tennis in the afternoon. I sat with Mama and had an amusing conversation with N.P. Papa, T, Anya and Rodionov played tennis. 11 degrees in the shade, 23 – in the sun. Had tea as usual. [It is] unbearable not to see S. for so long. 8 degrees in the evening. Sat with Mama. Anya pasted postcards. Papa read in his [room].

Tuesday. 22 October. There was obednya and a big breakfast. Shurik came over. Played 1 set with Papa, Anya and T. in the afternoon. Then N.P., Rodionov and Kozhevnikov came, and we walked, since Papa could not play because of his finger. Mama rode in a small equipage. Walked to the beach on the horizontal path through Oreanda and returned for tea. It was terribly nice to walk and talk to dear Shurik. At 6 o'cl. saw them off to the motor and bid our farewells twice. Did not see my S. At 10 in the evening we 2 went to the pier in Yalta in a closed motor with Mama, Anya, Ira, N.P. and Rodionov, then to the yacht and back home – [it was] nice. Papa read. 8 degrees, 32 degrees in the sun in the afternoon.

Wednesday. 23 October. Had the first painting lesson with N.P. Krasnov. At 8 in the morning Papa went hunting in Kosmodemyansk and returned after 6 in the

---

[205] Carriage drawn by a pair of horses.

evening. Had breakfast with Mama and Prince Trubetskoy. He feels well after surgery. In the afternoon we 4 went to Lower Massandra with Mama, Anya, Ira and Nastenka. Finally saw my S. with Kublitsky and Ippolit in the rose alley. Played different games: the sorcerer, cat-and-mouse and oskar. It was not that much fun for me. Was very happy to see S. Mama sat, walked, picked flowers. [We] stopped at a meadow where Aleksei was. They had tea, baked potatoes in charcoal and rolled around in hay. After dinner Papa read Teffi to us. Raining. 10 degrees. Helped Anya paste in the album. Mama read. She is tired. Shame that Shurik wasn't there.

Thursday. 24 October. We 2 went shopping in Yalta with Nastenka and Ira. Saw S. through the fieldglass. The officers of the 16th regiment had breakfast. Today is 35 years since Grandpapa became chief of the regiment. Papa has been in charge for 4 years, and Aleksei replaced him today. In the afternoon we 4 went to Ai-Todor with Papa and Mama. A, myself and Mama got into a motor. The rest walked all the way. Had tea with Aunt Ksenia, Irina and Felix. Nikita and Vasia[206] were there too. At 9 in the evening we 2 and Papa went to the new infantry barracks for a ball. Such fun! Danced 1 quadrille with the regimental commander Viranovsky, and 2 – with dear Shurik. What darling, in my favorite jacket. Everything was very cozy. All the dances [were] in one hall. Prince Trubetskoi led the 2nd quadrille, Viranovsky led the 1st. Returned at 11. Mama is tired, her back aches. 11 degrees.

---

[206] Nikita and Vasily were Olga's first cousins, the sons of Grand Duchess Ksenia.

Friday. 25 October. At 10 ½ Papa and we 2 went to Kosmodenyansk via Krasny Kamen. [It was] cold and foggy on the elevation. Aunt Ksenia, Aunt Minnie, Uncle Georgi, Irina and Felix were with us. Had a cold breakfast in the cabin. On the way back walked a mile in the mountains. Had tea with Papa and Mama. We were going to [see] a cinematograph after dinner, but had to postpone it because of V.A. Dedulin. Last night he started feeling sick after the ball, and is now dying. He received the last sacrament, and Mama and Papa were with him until 11.15. He fell asleep during the sacrament. They just returned. He was so touching the whole time. Saw boating exercises and S. from far away. May God keep him.

Saturday. 26 October. V.A. Dedulin died last night at a quarter to 12. At 2 o'clock we went there for the panikihda. The poor widow and children, so sad. Sonia Komarova had not arrived yet. Katia is here already. In the morning we 2 walked on the horizontal trail with Anya and [my] brother. N.P., S., Butakov and Nevyarovsky had breakfast. In the afternoon walked in the vineyard with Papa. Mama rode in a carriage. Had tea and dinner together. At 5.15 the body was brought out. The Svodny regiment, the escort and the police walked behind the coffin up to the Livadia church. Mama and the widow were in the carriage. There was a panikhida for the dear deceased. Saw Shurik from far away. Very warm. 14 degrees in the shade in the afternoon. 12 degrees in the evening. Mama was very tired of course.

Sunday. 27 October. Went to obednya and a big breakfast. Afterwards Mama went downstairs. Very windy. It poured at 7 in the morning. 8 degrees in the evening. In the afternoon we all walked to Oreanda and back with Mama in a carriage. Papa, N.P., Rodionov and S. walked with us. I walked with S. the entire time, it was so nice. Had tea with them and also with Aunt Ksenia, who took us both with Irina. They stayed with us until dinner. At 9 o'cl. went to the panikhida with Papa and Mama. Dear Shurik was at a meeting. Rained. A.'s temperature is normal. Aleksei's leg hurts.

Olga and Tatiana in Oreanda

Monday. 28 October. Had lessons. Kozhevnikov, Shepotiev, Batushka and Rodionov had breakfast. Did not see S. today. Played tennis in the afternoon. Lost 1 set with Anya against T. and Papa. Then played 2 sets with Papa against her and Rodionov, a tie. Then sat with N.P. and Mama. [I feel] so empty. [There is] not much foliage, but [is] warm. Had tea as usual, and with Kublitzky. A also came. Aleksei's leg hurts. In the evening went to the panikhida with Papa and Mama. Sonia Kazakova arrived. Dear Shurik was there. May the Lord keep him. 9 degrees.

Tuesday. 29 October. At 10 o'clock Papa, Mama and we 3 went to the burial, after which we walked behind the hearse up to the barracks, and Papa let the troops [walk] in front of him. Shurik stood with the Cossacks. Saw S. from the back. Very windy. On the way back, we let Papa and M. out and went to the vineyard from which we could see the entire procession. At 1 o'clock "The Proot" went out to the sea. Had breakfast and dinner with Papa and Mama. Tennis in the afternoon. Played a single with N.P. and tied. Lost 1 set with Papa against Rodionov and T. Mama also came. Had tea as usual. In the evening sat with Mama. Moon, wind, 5 degrees. Aleksei's leg still hurts, which was why he did not get dressed although he did have breakfast with us.

Wednesday. 30 October. Had lessons. Zlebov, Babitzyn, Kublitzky and Smirnov had breakfast. Tennis in the afternoon. Lost a set with N.P. against Rodionov and T, then played 2 sets with Papa against them and tied. Zborovsky and Shaprinsky also came over. Shame that Shurik wasn't there. By now I am used to S. not being here. Mama also came. Cold but not windy. 7 degrees in the afternoon. 5 1/2 degrees in the evening. Moon. Had tea as usual. In the evening played Kolorito with Mama. Papa read in his [room].

Thursday. 31 October. We 2, Nastenka and Ira went shopping in Yalta. Saw boating exercises and ran into Shurik. Stolitza, Butakov, Nevyarovsky and Ippolit had breakfast. Tennis in the afternoon. [I] won the American set with M. and Shurik. He got 5, she – 0. Then won with him against T. and Butakov: 7-5, then lost against him and M: 5-7. S. and Zborovsky played with Papa. Mama cut ribbons for the cotillion. Had tea as usual. I sat between my friends. Had dinner in the saloon on the yacht. Awfully cozy. After that – a cinematograph from [Odessa?] in the dining room upstairs. Funny and interesting. I sat next to my S. Mama was there too, thank God. Her leg aches. N.P. has a cold. Left at 12.10. The officers wore black uniforms.

~

November

Friday. 1 November. Had lessons. Walked with Nastenka and Ira. 14 degrees. Warm, nice. Shepotiev, Kozhevnikov, Batushka and my S. had breakfast. We planned to go to the yacht to meet the Greek Aunt Olga who was supposed to arrive on The Almar. [It was] chilly out at sea. She arrived in a motor, and Mama and Papa went to see her after dinner. Tennis in the afternoon. Lost 2 sets with Shurik against T. and Zborovsky. Won with M. against A. and Shurik: 5-7. Lots of fun. M. took group pictures. Laughed a lot. N.P. and Rodionov were there. Aleksei, too, but he left earlier. Mama cut ribbons. 11 degrees, 12 degrees in the evening. Tea as usual. Sat with Anya in the evening.

Saturday. 2 November. We 2 rode horses through Ai-Nikola, the farm and the Livadia settlement. Very warm, 15 degrees. N.P., Zlebov, Smirnov and Kublitzky had breakfast. Tennis in the afternoon. Played an American set with Shurik, and then 2 sets with him. Went to the yacht with Mama and had dinner in the large dining hall with the officers and suite. An awning was set up around the afterdeck and quarter-deck, with lights and green garlands. Some officers wore masks. Danced on the afterdeck and around the control cabin. [I] danced a quadrille with S. Very cozy, nice, fun. Then played a game twice. Palladino composed a march and played it. At first [I] danced with N.P. Left at 12.10. 11 degrees.

Author's note: Olga's 18th birthday was on November 3, 1913. There was no entry in her diary on that date.

Olga on the yacht, with a bouquet of flowers. Maria is on her right, Tatiana and Anastasia (with a camera) on her left.

Monday. 4 November. Had lessons until 11. After that walked to the beach through Oreanda with Mama in a carriage. Aleksei rode in a dvoika, we followed him and then we [rode] with him and Ioann Zlatoust[207]. It was so nice. Papa returned with us. S., Ippolit, Babitzyn and Stolitza had breakfast. Tennis in the

---

[207] Saint John Chrysostomos, the Archbishop of Constantinople

afternoon. Played a set with Papa against Zborovsky. Then played with T. against N.P. and A., won both. Then I played with S. against A. and Zborovsky, tied. Rodionov was also there. Tea as usual, sat with my S. Christopher[208] was also there. Mama is fine thank God. I hurt my left leg, and am limping. I fell on the stairs seeing the officers off. In the evening we 4 and Papa went to the theater and cinematograph. They showed an interesting [motion] pictures about conquering the Caucasus, and then a funny one. Shurik was there. Sat with Mama until 12 o'cl. 9 degrees. Chilly.

Tuesday. 5 November. Sat at Mama's until 11. Then had a lesson. I am pushed around in a wheelchair. Had breakfast upstairs with Mama and Aleksei, then came downstairs. N.P., Kublitzky, Batushka and Shepotiev came over. It is raining all day. 7 degrees in the evening. Stayed at home, pasted in albums. My S. helped me. N.P. and Stolitza were there too. Sat with S. at tea in the dining room. We 2 had dinner with Papa and Mama in Kharaks, also with Aunt Olga, Aunt Minnie, Uncle Georgi, Christopher and Bagration. Played cards in the evening, same as last time. Mama is tired.

Wednesday. 6 November. I am upstairs with Aleksei. Had lessons. They had breakfast downstairs with the hussars, Butakov, Zlebov, Kozhevnikov and Babitzyn. Tennis in the afternoon. I stayed home, had a healing mud application on my leg. Had had tea with everyone: N.P., Butakov, Shurik, Zborovsky. Dinner was downstairs at 7 in the evening. Masses of people. Mama came later, greeted

---

[208] H.R.H. Prince Christoforos of Greece, son of "Aunt Minnie.

everyone, and the ball started. T. and Anya opened it. I danced a quadrille with the warrant officer Delinkov, a cotillion – with PrinceTrubetskoy. Towards the end [I] waltzed with S. for a while. He danced with the Kleinmichels the entire time. The threesome was there: Shurik, Zborovsky and Ippolit. [It was] rather nice and merry. About 40 couples. [It] ended at 1 in the morning. 7 degrees.

Olga in Livadia

Thursday. 7 November. Got up late. At 10.15, we 4 and Papa went to "The Peter I" ship in Yalta. R.O.P.T very cozy. Inspected all the cabins. From there we went to the yacht. Papa greeted the crew. S. is on duty. Nevyarovsky, Stolitza, Smirnov and Kublitzky had breakfast. Tennis in the afternoon. I worked and then played downstairs. Papa, S., Zborovsky and Shurik played. Tea as usual. Cold. I sat between S. and Shurik. 6 1/2 degrees in the evening. Aleksei's arm aches, he is lying down. Mama is tired. Sat with her until 10 o'cl.

Friday. 8 November. Had lessons. Went shopping in Yalta with Ira. Cold but sunny. S., Butakov, Shepotiev, Ippolit and the Vilensky regiment officers had breakfast. It is a regimental holiday. [They] played tennis, I did not play [but] sat with Mama and N.P. First under the bushes, then on the court. Tea as usual, sat with S. and Shurik. We 2 and Papa went to Kharax for dinner. All the same [people] were there as last time. Played again. Returned at 11 1/2. 5 degrees. Mama is tired. Aleksei's arm still hurts.

Saturday. 9 November. Sat on the balcony for a ¾ of an hour in the sun. Mama did not sleep well, she is tired and her back aches. N.P., Zlebov, Batushka, Stolitza and 4 artillery officers had breakfast. The 1st brigade holiday. Tennis in the afternoon. I did not play. S., Shurik and Zborovsky were there. N.P. sat with Mama. I am cold. [Not as cold as?] yesterday, but still not warm. At tea [I] sat with S. and Shurik. Had dinner downstairs with the Emir of Bukhara. He is leaving tomorrow. Mama was also there. Went to vsenoshnaya. 6.5 degrees. Went to bed at 11 o'clock.

Sunday. 10 November. Obednya and a big breakfast. The Delegation of the 53rd Valensky infantry regiment came over. Mama did not come downstairs. She has a headache and is tired. Sat with her until 3.15 o'cl.. Then we 2 and Papa went to Princess Baryatinskaya's[209]. Danced a lot, it was such fun. Danced 3 waltzes with Sh. and 1 with S. N.P. arrived later. Papa played kosti. The cotillion was very interesting and merry. Danced the first quadrille with Mankovsky, the cotillion, 2 quadrilles and mazurka - with Kiriev. Returned at 7 o'cl. In the evening sat with Mama. 5 degrees.

Monday. 11 November. Had lessons. At 11 in the morning [I] soaked [my] feet in [hot water?] for 10 minutes at 30 degrees. Nevyarovsky, Babitzyn, Kozhevnikov and Smirnov had breakfast. Tennis in the afternoon. Played 2 sets with Sh. against T. and Zborovsky, a tie, then played with A. against Sh. and M., lost both, and finally played 1 set with our champion Count Sumarokov, against Papa and Rodionov, won 6-1. N.P. sat with Mama. Lonesome without S. We 2 had dinner with Papa and Mama at Kharax and in the evening played the same games with the same [people]. 6 degrees. Mama's headache is better but she feels tired.

Tuesday. 12 November. At 8 in the morning the yacht went out to sea to Feodosia and back to test the engine. At 3 o'clock it passed Livadia and saluted.

---

[209] Princess Maria Viktorovna Baryatinskaya was one of the Empresses maids of honor and friends.

[We] played tennis. Played 3 1/2 sets with A. against T. and M. We won 2, they won 1 1/2 sets. It was fun. Cold. 4 degrees. Mama was also there, as well as Zborovsky. Tea as usual. In the evening sat with Mama. 2 degrees. Went to bed at 11 ½ as usual.

Wednesday. 13 November. Freeze during the night. Had lessons and a turnip compress overnight. Kublitzky, Batushka, Rodionov and Ippolit had breakfast. The yacht reversed. Played 2 sets with A. against Sh. and M. and lost. After that [played] with them and with T., Papa, Anya, Zborovsky, and Rodionov ran around the tennis court and played. Lots of fun. Sh. is such a sweetheart. Mama also came. Cold. 3 degrees. N.P. had tea. I want [to see] S. Sat with Mama in the evening. Papa read about Suvorov[210]. 2 degrees at night.

Thursday. 14 November. Had a turnip compress as usual. Obednya at 11. Mama came and also had breakfast, also N.P., the commander, Butakov, Stolitza, Kozhevnikov, Smirnov. In the afternoon we 4 walked along Mama's carriage with Papa, Anya, N.P., Sh. and Rodionov. [It was] very nice and merry. Did not see S. After tea [saw] a cinematograph at 5 1/2. Mama left half way through [it]. Sh. also came, such a darling. In the evening sat with Mama. Papa read in his Navy jacket. 4 1/2 degrees.

Friday. 15 November. Had lessons, after that [we] went shopping for wool with Nastenka as usual. It rained in the morning, [was] wet. No sun in the afternoon.

[210] Alexander Vasielvich Suvorov: Russia's famous 18th century military commander

S., Rodionov, Zlebov and Shepotiev had breakfast. Papa received Mongolian ambassadors extraordinaire. Walked through the farm beside and behind Mama's carriage, Mon Jardin and Livadia. N.P., Rodionov and S. came along [with us]. I walked with darling S., [it was] so nice. Had tea all together. We 2, Papa and Mama went to Kharax for dinner. The same [people] were there and did the same things. Uncle Georgi – no, uncle Mitya – yes. Returned at 11 o'cl 20 min. 5 1/2 degrees.

Olga, Maria and Tatiana with with their mother in Livadia

Saturday. 16 November. At 10 in the morning we two and Papa went to the cape in Yalta. Walked through the yacht. Papa greeted the crew. Then went in 1 motor (Babitzyn) to the rope boat The Uraletz. It rocked on the waves. [We] inspected the boat and returned. Papa did the testing on deck. Nice. N.P., Butakov, Nevyarovsky and Smirnov had breakfast. Rain. Sat at home and pasted in albums. S. helped me. N.P. and Stolitza were here. Nevyarovsky, Zlebov and Drenteln played kosti with Papa. Had tea all together. Mama has a headache. Went to vsenoshnaya and had dinner downstairs. 7 degrees. Wet. High surf. [All] is well.

Sunday. 17 November. Obednya at 11. Had breakfast upstairs after that, with Papa, Mama, Aunt Olga, Aunt Minnie and Christopher. In the afternoon [we] walked through Oreanda and Kurpaty beside Mama's carriage with Papa, N.P., Anya and dear S. Had tea all together. At 7 in the evening had a big dinner, and after that [there was] a ball until 12 o'cl. 20 min. Such fun, so nice and amusing. 1 quadrille with Knyazhevich, 2 – with S., cotillion, mazurka, etc. – with Sh. Enjoyed it enormously. S. is kind and affectionate. 4 degrees. Masses of people. Paladino played.

Monday. 18 November. Got up late. Bekker. M. Gilliard read to me and T. The 14th Divison officers had breakfast on the occasion of 60th anniversary of the Battle of Sinop. From the yacht [the following] came: S., Babitzyn, Batushka and

Ippolit. 24 degrees in the sun, 10 1/2 degrees in the shade. Tennis in the afternoon. Sumarokov, Anya, Zborovsky, Rodionov and Sh. played with Papa. I sat with N.P. and Mama, whose heart is 1 1/2, and aches around the rib cage. Had tea as usual. Went to bed at 10 o'cl.

Tuesday. 19 November. Stayed in bed until 11. Got up only at 8 1/2 to greet Papa, who was leaving for a hike at Ayudag and then Kurpaty. [...] Mama sat in an easy chair in her robe. We 4 and Aleksei had breakfast with her. In the afternoon [we] walked through Livadia settlement and the farm with N.P., Sh., Rodionov, Kozhevnikov and Anya. Mama [rode] in her carriage. Nice. Did not see S. Played dobchinsky-bobchinsky with them in the dining room until tea. Papa returned for tea. In the evening sat with Mama, worked. 7 degrees.

Wednesday. 20 November. Had lessons. Butakov, Kublitzky, Shepotiev and Smirnov had breakfast. Tennis in the afternoon. Won 2 sets with A. against Sh. and M. and won 1 set with Sh. against M. and Zborovsky. Rodionov and Sumarokov were also there. N.P. sat with Mama. 5 degrees. Tea and dinner as usual. Went to vsenoshnaya. In the evening worked with Mama. Papa read in his [room]. Lonesome – have not seen S. 5 degrees.

Thursday. 21 November. Went to obednya. The Border Guard and Semenovsky regiment holiday. The officers had breakfast. Tennis in the afternoon. Won 2 sets with A. against M. and Butakov, then won 1 set against them with M., and then lost a set with her against T. and A. Sumarokov and Zborovsky were also there. N.P. sat with Mama. Around 2 o'cl. Mama received the ladies, and we were there too. She has a headache. Tea as usual. Pink sunset. Boring. Did not see S. or Sh., who is on duty. We 2 had dinner with Papa at Kharax. All the same, and ncle Georgi returned. Also played writing games. Returned at about 12 o'cl. 7 degrees.

Friday. 22 November. Had lessons and went shopping in Yalta with Nastenka. S., N.P., Zlebov and Stolitza had breakfast. I was so happy to see him[211], but also had a heavy heart for some reason. Foolish. Tennis in the afternoon. Won 2 sets with Sumarokov against Papa and Anya. Then won 2 sets with A. against Sh. and M. and won 1 set with Sh. against A. and Zborovsky. Rodionov was there. N.P. sat with Mama. Had tea with them as usual, as well as dinner.

---

[211] Voronov?

"We 4"

Saturday. 23 November. We 2 went shopping in Yalta with Nastenka and Ira. Ran into Sh., but of course did not see S.. The 5th Lithuanian Infantry Regiment Officers had breakfast because of their regiment holiday, also 10 officers from the Pavlovsky regiment and 3 Cossack hetmans. Mama came downstairs. Tennis in the afternoon. 8 degrees but chilly. Lost 1 set with A. against M and T, then played with N.P. against A. and T., a tie. And finally lost against T. and Zborovsky with M: 4-6. Sumarokov and Rodionov played with Papa. Tea as usual, dinner downstairs. Went to vsenoshnaya. Mama came downstairs after dinner. 7 1/2 degrees.

Sunday. 24 November. Obednya at 11 and a big breakfast. Afterwards Mama came downstairs. [It] drizzled a little. We 4 went to the Lower Massandra with Papa and Mama. Mama brought her carriage, and we walked along the Rose Alley with N.P. and Rodionov. A little after 4 o'cl. [we] went to the yacht. Stayed there. [It was awfully nice. At about 5 o'cl. [we] went to the saloon and had tea there with the remaining officers. [It was] so cozy, but [it was] such a shame that S. was not there. The crew returned from the cinematograph accompanied by music. At 6 o'cl. Mama, Anya and I went to the Red Cross Sanatorium. It was very nice. All [patients] there have tuberculosis. Returned at 7 o'cl. Ran into Sh. at the waterfront. Stopped by Trina's. In the evening sat with Mama. 6 or 7 degrees.

Monday. 25 November. Had lessons. At 11 o'clock we 2 and Nastenka went to see Countess Apraksina. She has been in bed for a month already. I think it is appendicitis. Played with the children. Gertelman from the artillery unit had breakfast, also Kozhevnikov, Babitzyn, Nevyarovsky and S. from the yacht. It was good and not good at the same time, to see him. [I] did not say a word to him, and don't want to. In the afternoon [I] watched the rehearsals of tomorrow's parade. Dear Sh. was there. Papa, Mama, N.P. and Anya played kosti. We 4 played hide-and-seek downstairs with Kublitzky and Kozhevnikov in the dark. Rain. We 2 and Papa went to Kharax for dinner. Played writing games. 7 degrees. Returned after 12 o'cl. Mama was still up.

Tuesday. 26 November. Moleben at 11, and a parade after that. Rodionov was with the platoon, Sh. – with the escort. Overcast. The St George's medal holders and the lower-ranks had breakfast in the tent. The officers ate with us. In the afternoon walked in the vineyards and Oreanda with Papa, Anya, Sh., Rodionov and Babitzyn, hiked up the [illeg.] hill. It was drizzling the whole time. Mama and N.P. stayed home. Her heart is 2 and she is tired. Had tea and dinner as usual. In the evening played kolorito with Mama. Papa read in his [room]. 3 1/2 degrees. I don't even know if I am sad about not seeing S.

Wednesday. 27 November. Had lessons. Kublitzky, Rodionov, Smirnov and Ippolit had breakfast. At 2 o'cl. Mama and Drobyazchin baptized Vasily, the son of V.D. Yuritzyn from the Crimean regiment. He screamed a lot. Such a darling. After that we went to play tennis. Won 2 sets with A. against Sh. and M., then won 1 set with Sh. against N.P. and A., and then another one against them. Zborovsky, Sumarokov and Rodionov were there too. Papa's shin hurts and he is limping. Mama also came. Had tea and dinner as usual. Did not see S. In the evening sat with Mama. Aleksei's leg hurts. 3 degrees. Mama came by our bedroom when we were already in bed. She was at Aleksei's before that.

Thursday. 28 November. Walked to Yalta with Nastenka. 35 m. [It was] damp and muddy. N.P., Kozhevnikov, Shepotiev, Nevyarovsky had breakfast. Papa and Mama rode in the afternoon since Papa's leg still hurts. We 4 went to

Oreanda on the horizontal trail and down with Anya, N.P. and Kozhevnikov. When we returned [we] played hide-and-seek in the dark with Sh. and Kozhevnikov. It was lots of fun. The rest of them played kosti upstairs. Had tea all together. Everyone from Kharax and Kichkin had dinner. After that we wrote. Mama is tired. Aleksei is sleeping. 8 degrees.

Olga and her sisters with officers

Friday. 29 November. Had lessons. At 10 o'clock A., Trina and I went shopping in Yalta [walking] through puddles and mud. Kublitzky, Butakov, Ippolit and Batushka had breakfast. Stayed at home in the afternoon. Papa and Mama played kosti with N.P. and Anya. Played hide-and-seek downstairs with Sh.,

Zborovsky and Rodionov. It was lots of fun. Romped around a lot. Had tea at 5 or

a little earlier. At 9 o'clock we 4 and Papa went to the Town Theater for a charity

play. It was arranged by Princess Baryatinskaya. The first part took place in an

abandoned cabin, then – cinematograph. Very beautiful. Thank God [I] finally

saw S., albeit just in passing. He was at the cinematograph. Sh. was also at the

theater, he wore his jacket with a black cloak, same as during the day. Returned

at about 11.15, before the show ended. Poor Aleksei is crying, [as] his leg hurts.

Mama's heart is 2, she is tired.

"… Batushka had breakfast." Rare photo of Olga and Tatiana with a priest.

Saturday. 30 November. Went to Yalta with Nastenka and Ira. [It was] muddy and slippery. We 5 had breakfast with Mama and Papa upstairs. Aleksei's right leg still hurts. He is crying and not eating, the poor darling. At 2 1/2 Aunt Olga came over to say good bye. We 2 and Papa took her to the pier, where she got on The Almaz and sailed out to sea. It is foggy and drizzling. Meanwhile we went to the yacht. Papa greeted the crew, who were lined up outside under the tent, so that he would not have to walk around with his bad leg. We went to the deck-bridge, where we could watch The Almaz, which saluted as it passed Livadia. The commander served us coffee in the navigation cabin. There were regimental maneuvers on the pier. S. was there too. Stopped by to see Stolitza, who is in bed with water in his knee, and went to the saloon. The officers arrived at 3 1/2. N.P. played kosti with Papa, Mama and Anya. We played hide-and-seek with S., T., Zborovsky and Rodionov downstairs in the dark. It was lots of fun. Had tea as usual. Mama stayed for only 20 minutes because Aleksei was in bed in her room. He played cards with her while we went to church. Had dinner with everyone. Mama's heart is 1 1/2, she has a headache and is tired. Went to bed at about 11 o'cl. 5 degrees. Rain.

~

December

Sunday. 1 December. Had a turnip compress at night. Obednya, big breakfast. N.P. arrived at 3 o'cl, he played kosti with Papa, Mama and Anya. Sh., Rodionov, Kozhevnikov and Zborovsky played hide-and-seek with us downstairs. First [I] sat with Aleksei, he did not sleep well, but felt fine in the afternoon. We played with him cheerfully and had tea. Mama's heart is 1-1/2,[she] does not feel well. We 4 and Papa went to the yacht saloon for dinner. S. was on duty, [I] saw him through the hatch. Then [we] watched a cinematograph in the dining room. Nice and funny. Then S. came in at the last moment. I was very happy, kept waiting for him so long but then, I don't know, [I] got nervous. Did not leave until 12 1/2, because the motor did not come. Rained hard. 5 degrees. Mama was still up.

Monday. 12 December. At 9.15 in the morning, we 2 and Papa went to Ai-Danil for a children's sanatorium consecration by the sea and on the border with Gurzuf. Returned at about 11.45. Rodionov, Batushka, Smirnov and Nevyarovsky had breakfast. After that Grigori Yefimofich's wife Praskovya and Varya went to Mama's, [they] sat together for a while. At 3 1/2 N.P. arrived, played kosti with Papa, Mama and Anya as usual. S., Rodionov, Sh. and Zborovsky first went downstairs to see Aleksei, then [we] played hide-and-seek. Sh. and M. were searching the entire time and could not find everyone – it was time for tea. S. is so sweet, and Sh. is also nice. It was fun. We 2 and Papa had dinner in Kharaks. Then played the same games. All is well. Returned at 11 o'cl. 20 min. 5 degrees. Rain. Aleksei is sleeping.

Tuesday. 3 December. At 9 1/2 went to Yalta with Shura to see the dentist Kostritsky. It was pouring [rain] all day. Passed by the yacht. N.P. was peering from the scuttle, and S. leaped out on deck. N.P., Shepotiev, Babitzyn and Kozhevnikov had breakfast. At 2 1/2, we 4 went to the Red Cross sanatorium in 2 motors with Anya and Ira, saw all the patients. A very nice day. N.P. and Nevyarovsky arrived at 4 o'clock. They played kosti with Anya and Papa. Mama got up only for tea since her heart is 2 1/2 and she is tired. We played hide-and-seek with Sh., Rodionov and Zborovsky, such fun. Sh. is [wearing] his dark good jacket as usual, and an overcoat. Aleksei feels better – it is resolving but his leg is swollen now, and the temperature at night was 38.2. 6 1/2 degrees. Went to bed at 10 o'cl. Papa read. We chose gifts for the staff.

Wednesday. 4 December. Had lessons. Rodionov, Kublitzky, Ippolit and Batushka had breakfast. In the afternoon walked through the vineyards, etc. with Papa, Anya, Sh., Kublitzky and Zborovsky, returned at 3 1/2. N.P. sat with Mama. Her heart is not as enlarged, but she is tired and has a headache. When we returned, [we] played hide-and-seek cheerfully. Sh. [is wearing] his good jacket, terribly nice. Had tea and dinner as usual. Did not see S. Clear, sunny, blue sky, snow in the mountains. In the evening Aleksei's temperature was 38.1. Natasha Karlova died of pneumonia. In the evening [we] sorted out gifts with

281

Mama. Papa read. Around 4 degrees. Saw Praskovya Fedorovna and Varya at Anya's at 6 o'clock.

Thursday. 5 December. Went to see Kostritzky with Shura. Walked on the pier, saw N.P. from far away. My S., Butakov, Nevyarovsky and Prince Golitzyn (cricket) had breakfast. Rehearsal of tomorrow's parade was at 3 o'cl. S. marched. We 4, Sh. and Zborovsky played hide-and-seek downstairs in a few rooms, in the dark of course. Ran around, crawled on all fours, pushed furniture. Very nice and fun. N.P., Nevyarovsky and Dmitri just arrived and played kosti with Papa. Mama sat nearby. She got up late, her heart is 2-1/2, not good. Aleksei is fair. Rain. Around 6 in the evening she received the Cossacks and our 2 friends. Went to vsenoshnaya. Went to bed at 10 o'cl. 3 degrees. Aleksei's temperature is 37.9.

Friday. 6 December. Had a turnip compress. The parade [was] at 10 1/2. S. marched. Then obednya and a big breakfast. He was there, also other relatives. I congratulated Papa while he was still in bed. Mama did not come downstairs, her heart is not good, headache, and [she] feels badly in general. Aleksei was merry in the afternoon, in the evening [he] fell fast asleep. 37.5. At 3.15 [we] played hide-and-seek with T. and Zborovsky. Fun, nice, wonderful as usual. Had tea with them, Papa, Mama, Anya and N.P. We 4 had dinner with Papa and Dmitri in the yacht saloon. S. is on duty of course. I missed him a lot. [code: "my darling turtledove"]²¹². Then [we] went into the control cabin and greeted the crew through the window. Strong wind. The yacht rocked and was pushed closer to the pier. Force 8. ½ degree. [We] danced downstairs in the green dining room, played turkey and charades. [It was] such fun. But I wish S. was here. He came after 12 o'cl, and we left at 12.15. Mama is lying down, she has severe headache. We brought N.P. with us. Paladino.

Saturday. 7 December. Went with Shura to see Kostritsky. Rode along the pier. Saw S., he was on duty. Picked up T. and Nastenka and returned. Zlebov, Ippolit, Babitzyn and S. had breakfast. [Code: "[my] affectionate, precious, [he] smiled and was happy, the dear turtledove"]. It is snowing all day, the ground, etc. is white. In the afternoon first played hide-and-seek with Sh., Zborovsky and Rodionov, then – the charades. Went upstairs and continued playing very happily. Had tea as usual with N.P. and Dmitri. Went to vsenoshnaya. Had dinner downstairs. The Spanish ambassador Veniaza and his wife were there. After that sat with Mama. She has a headache and is tired. Aleksei's temperature was 37 in the evening. Dmitri talked nonsense. 1 1/2 degrees.

---

²¹² Olga wrote in her special code language when she wished to say something private.

Tatiana, Olga and Anastasia looking at an album

Sunday. 8 December. Before obednya stayed with Mama as usual. Big breakfast. In the afternoon A, T, myself and Anya walked in Oreanda and returned by 3 1/2. Incredibly windy and very cold. When we returned [we] played the charades upstairs with M, Sh., T, A, Rodionov and Zborozsky. Fun. N.P. played kosti with Papa, Mama and Dmitri. Had tea all together. At 2 o'cl said goodbye to Praskovya Fedorovna and Varya. I feel lonesome without S. We 2 had dinner with Dmitri and Papa in Kharaks. 2 degrees below. When we returned, it was 2 degrees, there was snow on the ground. The same were there and played the same games. [It was] not that much fun for me. Mama was going to take a bath. She had a headache in the afternoon.

Monday. 9 December. Had lessons. At 11 in the morning we 2 and Nastenka went shopping in Yalta. It was pouring [rain]. We stopped by the pier. Saw N.P. peering out of the scuttle. The Turkish ambassador, Kozhevnikov, Shepotiev, Nevyarovsky and Smirnov had breakfast. At 2 o'cl. 20 min., we 2 and Anya went to the Muzlarsky Sanatorium on the hill. All tuberculosis patients there, including our boatswain Ivanov and Natasha from the beach. It was nice. Blizzard and strong wind. When we returned [we] played charades with Sh., M., and A. T. played with Zborovsky and Kublitzky. Lots of fun. Had tea as usual. Aleksei's temperature was 37.5 in the evening. Did not see S. In the evening sat with Mama. 3 degrees. Rain. The wind finally calmed down—it was really blustering hard earlier.

Olga with her two youngest sisters and officers

Tuesday. 10 December. Last visit to the dentist with Shura. Stopped by the pier. Saw N.P. and my S. on duty. N.P., Kublitzky, Stolitza and Batushka had breakfast. In the afternoon we 3, Papa and Dmitri walked on the horizontal trail, hiked up the Cross Hill and the rocks. Very fun. Smoked. Wonderful weather. 7 degrees. The terrible storm at night tore down the cypress trees near Papa's window. M. stayed with Mama. Anya left. Had dinner at a quarter to 8, and in 1 hour we 2 went to Narodny Dom with Papa and Dmitri to see the play A Life for the Tsar. It was fantastic. N.P., Sh. and S. were there, but I felt sad for some reason. Mama was still up. 5 degrees. Returned at 11.45.

11 December. Veselkin (was discharged from hospital). Had lessons. We 4 had breakfast in Kichkin with Papa and Dmitri. Inspected the rooms and [saw] Teymuraz. [From] there went to Kharax. Returned at 3 o'clock and walked in Oreanda and our Livadia vineyards. Mama [rode] in her carriage, for the first time in 2 weeks. Wonderful weather – sunny, 10 degrees in the shade. Papa, N.P., S., Sh. and Zborovsky also came. [I] walked with Sh. the whole time, and also sat with him at tea, also with S., and again [had] a strange feeling. Then – the charades. I played with A., Sh. and Zborovsky. T. – with M. and my S. Had dinner in Kharaks, then played the same games. Returned at 12 o'cl. 9 degrees. Mama just went to bed.

"We two"

Thursday. 12 December. Sat with Mama until 11 o'cl. because of the rain, [it]

kept pouring almost the entire day. S., Butakov, Shepotiev and Zlebov had

breakfast. At 2 o'cl. 15 min. we 2 and Nastenka went to the Red Cross

Sanatorium to bid farewell to the dear patients. Returned by half past 3. N.P. was

pasting in the album with Papa after he returned from a walk with Mama. We

played dobchinsky-bobchinsky and "suitcase" with T., Zborovsky and S. [code : "I

loved him terribly much, and it was so hard, I was angry and almost did not speak to him"] Had tea and dinner as usual. Saw the darling Shaprinsky children. Went to bed at about 11 o'cl. 8 degrees.

Friday. 13 December. Had lessons at 9 and 11 in the morning. At 10 o'clock Ira and I went to the Livadia hospital to [see] 4 patients, including the constable of 2nd category Popov, [who has] appendicitis. Kozhevnikov, Smirnov, Babitzyn and Ippolit had breakfast. [It] started raining. 10 degrees. Charades in the afternoon. I was with A. and S., [felt] nervous again for some reason [code: "someone else's and not mine, but still extremely loved"]. T [was] with M and Zborovsky. Dear Sh. did not come. He is sick and has an earache. Papa played kosti with Mama, N.P. and Zlebov. Had tea all together. In the evening we 4 went to the theater with Papa and Dmitri, color [motion] pictures, and cinematograph. After [we] returned, sat with Mama and then went to bed at 12 [o'cl]. 2 degrees.

When she wanted to say something private, Olga used a special code she devised - this is an example of the code in her 1913 diary. She used this code most often towards the end of the year, when she learned that Pavel Voronov - her "beloved S." - got engaged to be married to Olga Kleinmichel.

Saturday. 14 December. We 2 and Nastenka went shopping in Yalta. While we were at Zembinsky's S. walked by. [It is] warm in the sun. Zlebov, Stolitza, Batushka and S. had breakfast. Finally my real [code: "loved one"], although [I] think I said 1 1/2 words later, but still. May the Lord keep him. In the afternoon [we] walked through the settlement and the farm – muddy and swampy. N.P., Zborovsky and Kozhevnikov. Poor Sh. is still in bed, he is running a fever. Had tea as usual. Went to Kichkin and Kharax for dinner and vsenoshnaya. [We] played the piano. 4 degrees in the evening. Aleksei rode to Massandra.

Sunday. 15 December. Sat at Mama's until obednya as usual. Big breakfast. Sh. has an ear abscess, he is in bed. It's a shame I did not see him on my last day. Mama came downstairs later. In the afternoon [I] went to Oreanda with Mama, Papa, N.P., Zborovsky and Kozhevnikov. Had tea as usual. At 6 o'clock we 2 and Ira went to the Alexander III Sanatorium, where Peter Sheremetiev is a patient. [There are] 80 patients total. Nice. Walked on the pier. N.P. was peering from the scuttle. Had dinner with Papa and Mama. Dmitri is in Kharaks. 3 degrees.

The Standart Yacht. Monday. 16 December. Bekker. At 9.45 went to the orphanage for the chronically ill with T. and Nastenka. We reviewed it and returned. At 12 o'cl. a farewell moleben was held. Mama came. Had breakfast afterwards. Butakov, Shepotiev, Nevyarovsky and Kublitzky were there. After that Papa thanked the troops, they shouted "hurrah" and marched in review. At 3.45 went to the yacht in 2 carriages. Masses of people in the streets. Had tea in the dining room with the officers. Had dinner with them and Mama. I dictated log entries to S. in the lower control room, and we sat together. Awfully nice to be here. In the evening sat in the cozy space between the chimney and telegraph as usual and talked to my S. He went to bed a bit after 11 o'cl. because his watch

duty starts at 4 in the morning. N.P. sat with Mama on quarter-deck. Papa played

kosti. T. and Rodionov were there too. Went to bed at 11 1/2. 7 ¾ degrees.

Alma[213]. 10.06. Tuesday. 17 December. Sailed out to sea at 5 in the morning.

The yacht rocked a little, nice. Arrived in Sevastopol at 8.35 and docked.

Salutations. I was in the control room with S., Rodionov and Kublitzky. At 10 in

the morning Papa went to consecrate something at the aviation school. We were

there too until breakfast at 12 1/2. In the afternoon Mama was lying down on the

quarter deck. Very warm and a warm wind. Her heart is 2 1/2. In the afternoon

[we] took lots of pictures on the deck. Then sat in control room with my [code:

"loved one"] S., he wrote in the log journal, and we stayed there. He does not feel

well – headache and cough. It is so nice to be with him. Papa returned after 4

o'cl. Had tea with all the officers at 5 o'cl. Then went to look at the train with N.P.,

S., Rodionov and Ippolit. I sat on the deck, but S. did not come. Extremely sad. A

molebna was held on the deck at 7.40. After that the officers and the crew lined

up on the wharf, we bid our farewells and left. [It was] terribly hard. 13 degrees.

The yacht illuminated our way with searchlights. Went to bed at 10 o'cl. Mama is

already in bed. May the Lord save everyone and S.

Wednesday. 18 December. Sat with Mama and worked. Same in the afternoon.

We 4 also played with Dmitri. 6 degrees in the morning. 3 degrees below in the

evening. Mama has a headache but her heart is not enlarged, and she stayed in

---

[213] A small Crimean river which flows into the Black Sea.

bed all day. Aleksei went out during stops. Papa received noblemen in Orel. Ate with everyone. Lonesome without all the friends, the yacht, and of course S. Went to bed at 9.55. S. left Sevastopol for Petersburg.

Tsarskoe Selo. Thursday. 19 December. 17 degrees below in the morning, everything is covered with snow. Sat with Mama, worked, read, sang. Had breakfast and tea with everyone. At 6 ½ [we] arrived in Tsarskoe [Selo]. A molebna was held in Aleksei's new room. Dmitri, Grandmama, Aunt Olga, Aunt Ksenia and Irina had dinner with Papa and Mama. They left at 10 o'cl. Anya came over. Went to bed at 11 o'cl. Mama is awfully tired, her voice [sounds] faint. May God save us. I am not as lonesome but still want to see S. at times.

Olga and Tatiana with their father, Aunt Olga (left), Aunt Ksenia and Uncle Sandro

Friday. 20 December. Unpacked. Mama slept fine. Heart is not enlarged although she is tired. Count Grabbe had breakfast. Mama also sat at the table. In the afternoon we 4 and Papa walked to Znamenie and then through the garden. Mama [rode] in a carriage. Lots of snow. Ran into Aleksei in a sled and others. Had tea with Mama and Papa as usual. Papa went to Petersburg for dinner, we stayed home with Mama, Anya and Ira. Went to bed at 10 1/2. 2 degrees. My S. arrived today. May the Lord save him and help him.

Saturday. 21 December. We 4 and Trina rode to Pavlovsk in a sleigh. Then – [to a] clothing fitting. Uncle Boris[214], Count Sheremetiev, Count Fredericks and Aunt Olga had breakfast. Aunt Olga came over at 12 o'cl. In the afternoon [we] walked with her and Papa. It is snowing. Had tea and dinner with Mama, Papa and Aunt Olga. Went to Vsenoshnaya at the regimental church. 4 degrees below. Mama also came, but remained in the chapel. In the evening [we] sorted out the gifts for the officers. Aunt Olga is staying overnight in our room. I found out that S. [code: "My S. is marrying Olga Kleinmichel. May the Lord send him happiness, to my beloved S. So hard. So sad. May he be happy"].

Sunday. 22 December. At 11 o'clock we 5 and Papa went to the manege in 2 carriages for the 148th Kaspiysky regiment parade. Aleksei and Papa walked by the rows. Then – a big breakfast at the Grand Palace. At 3.07, we 2 and Nastenka went to Aunt Ksenia's in Petersburg for Irina and Felix's engagement party. Grandmama, Aunt Olga and others were there, [we] had tea. At 6 o'clock [we] went to [see] Countess Hendrikova and then – to the Winter Palace to [see] Count Geidel , angina and heart [disease]. Returned at 7 o'cl. 20 min. Had dinner with Papa and Mama, after that [we] chose vases for the relatives. Mama is very tired. May the Lord save S. 13 degrees below.

---

[214] H.I.H. Grand Duke Boris Vladimirovich of Russia, Nicholas II's first cousin.

Olga in the garden at Tsarskoe Selo

Monday. 23 December. At 10 o'clock we 2 and Anya went to see her niece
Tatiana, T.'s goddaughter. After that, walked in the garden with Trina, M., and A.
Very cold, 13 or 14 degrees below. Mordvinov had breakfast. In the afternoon
[we] decorated the [Christmas] tree. Had tea and dinner with Mama and Pmapa.
Helped Mama with the gifts until 7 pm. She is awfully tired, got almost no rest, in
addition Lili Obolenskaya came to see her. Went to bed at 11. At 6 o'cl. the
beaming and happy S. came over to Anya's. Thank you, Lord. 9 degrees.

295

Tuesday. 24 December. At 11 o'clock we 4, Mama and Papa went to the regimental church. Had breakfast all together, the same had dinner and Anya. At 2 o'clock [we] went to [see] Trina, Lili Obolenskaya and Sonya Orbeliani with Christmas trees and gifts. At 3 o'clock [we] went to [see] the servants. Mama came too, even though she was extremely tired. She did not go for so many years. Our Christmas party was at 4 ¼ in the playroom. We received many nice gifts from Papa and Mama: a sapphire ring, a long aquamarine broach, etc. At 5 o'cl. 50 min. we 4 and Papa went to Petersburg for Vsenoshnaya and then to dinner and a Christmas party at Grandmama's. Aunt Olga and Aunt Ksenia with [her] family were there. Returned at about 11. It has been a week since we left the yacht and I have not seen S.

Wednesday. 25 December. Christmas. At 11 went to obednya and moleben with Papa, then had breakfast. At 2 o'cl. we 5, Papa and Mama went to the manege for the Escort regiment's Christmas party. First we gave out gifts. Mama did that only in the beginning. She has not gone to this for a few years. The soldiers played the balalaikas, the Cossacks sang. Sh. is even more charming now. Talked to him and others, and was very glad to see him. Tea and dinner with Papa, Mama and Anya. [I] read and wrote letters. 12 degrees below.

Thursday. 26 December. We 4 walked with Trina. Very cold. 15 degrees below in the evening. I was reading a lot: "Perelom"[215] by Markevich. Had breakfast with Papa, Mama and Prince B-B. At 2 o'cl. we 5 went to another Christmas party with Papa and Aunt Olga, took turns giving out gifts. Dear Sh. was there. Talked to him and others. After that the Cossacks danced the lezginka, so wonderful. Had tea with Papa and Mama. Had dinner with Mama, she stayed at home, not to overstress herself. She does not feel well in cold weather: she cannot breathe. Her heart is not enlarged even though she had chest pains in the morning. Papa bid farewell to the Austrian ambassador. We stayed downstairs until 11. Played kolorito, etc. with Mama. Anya was here.

Friday. 27 December. At 10.20 in the morning we 4 and Nastenka went to the nanny school's Christmas party. Played with the children for a long time. Uncle Kostya had breakfast. In the afternoon we 4 walked. Blizzard, cold. Had tea in Papa's big study with Aunt Miechen and Uncle Kyrill. Dmitri had dinner with us. Mama is fine, thank God. 8 degrees below, the trains are running late. Sat with Mama until 11 o'cl.

Saturday. 28 December. Sat at home, wrote, read. Mama is [feeling] fair, she slept. At 12 1/2, the Metropolitan and the monks came over to glorify Christ. After that – breakfast. Aunt Olga and Uncle Petya. At 3.15 [we] walked with Papa and Aunt Olga. It was snowing. Not true [?]. At 4 ½ there was a Christmas party for the officers in the hall. Talked to the Svodny regiment, the Cossacks and Sh., [it

---

[215] "Breakdown"

was] fun and awkward. Then – tea, vsenoshnaya and dinner. Mama came to all of it. Thank God. Aunt Olga left at 10 in the evening. Played kolorito with Mama. Went to bed at 11 o'cl. 16 degrees below.

Sunday. 28 [sic] December. 20 degrees below in the morning. Went to obednya with Papa and Mama. Aleksei went too. Then – a big breakfast. Mama came over later. At 2.07, we 4 and Nastenka went to Petersburg. First to Grandmama's at the Anichkov, and from there at 3.10 – with Aunt Olga to her [house]. Sat and talked to Sh., Zborovsky, Yuzik, Vasily, Sklyarov and Vyacheslav Vasilievich Beliy. Had tea with the Cossacks. Listened to Herman Leuchtenberg with Sasha and Kolya, the marksman Kultnev, the officers Shinchin, Kulikovsky, Marie Claire, Kassikovskaya, Irina, Andryusha, Fedor and Felix. Then went to the hall and played cheat, turkey, etc. Then we 4, Sh., Zborovsky, Yuzik and Smirnov played the charades on stage. It was terribly amusing and nice. Then played the charades again. Had dinner at 7 o'cl. I was with Sh., then Aunt Olga, Prince Shternberg, Marie Claire, Yurik, T., Beliy, M., Zborovsky, and A. At 8.35 [we] left with Olga Yevgenievna. It was such fun. Very cold. Sat with Mama. She is fine, thank God. Stopped by Aleksei's. Papa read. Went to bed at 11 o'cl. Today is U.'s [?] birthday. May God save him.

Monday. 30 December. We 4 walked. Cold. Aunt Mavra had breakfast. Mama is well, thank God. At 4.10, we 4 and Olga Yevgenievna went to see Grandmama at Anichkov in Petersburg. Had tea upstairs with her, Aunt Olga and Aunt Ksenia.

At 5 1/2 went downstairs for the Christmas party in the hall. First Grandmama gave out presents to the officers, then – to the lower ranks. We talked to the Cossacks, they are so charming, especially my Sh. It ended at 6 1/2. We helped Aunt Olga get dressed and left at 7.15. It was so nice. Had dinner with Papa and Mama and sat until 11 o'cl. Papa read. 11 degrees below.

Tuesday. 31 December, 1913. We 4 took a walk and walked up the hill. Ioannchik had breakfast. At 3 o'cl. we 2 and Papa went to the military hospital for a Christmas party, after that – to the hussar regiment. Very nice. Lots of patients. Had tea and dinner with Papa and Mama. In the evening at 6 [we] went to Trina's, read fortunes. At 11 o'clock had tea with Papa and Mama, and greeted the New Year at the regimental church. I thank God for everything. Blizzard. 9 degrees below.

~

Additional books by Helen Azar

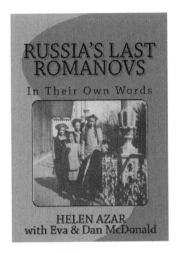

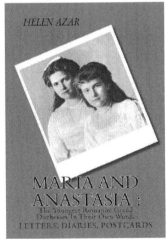